Freemasonry Fun Facts

What a Brother Knows

Peter Solomon

Table of Contents

Freemasonry Fun Facts 1 to 99 5

Freemasonry Fun Facts 100-199 29

Freemasonry Fun Facts 200-299 53

Freemasonry Fun Facts 300-399 79

Freemasonry Fun Facts 400-400 105

Freemasonry Fun Facts 500-599 125

Freemasonry Fun Facts 600-653 155

About the Author – Peter Solomon 171

Other books by Abrandax Publishing / Abrandax Media: 173

Freemasonry Fun Facts 1 to 99

1. The Bible is the most important book a Masonic student can study.

2. The Bible was originally written in Hebrew, Chaldian, Greek and Latin. Christ spoke Aramaic language; however the New Testament was written in Greek, and Abraham originally came from Chaldea.

3. The Bible must always be placed on the altar in a Masonic Lodge.

4. The Holy Bible is not mentioned in the Constitutions of 1723.

5 The Bible is first mentioned as a Great Light in Masonry circa 1760.

6. The first of the Old Charges, published in 1723 reads as: "A Mason is obliged by his tenure to obey the moral law; and if he rightly understands the art, he will never be a stupid atheist, nor an irreligious libertine".

7. Quatuor Coronatum, No. 2076 is the most eminent research Lodge in Masonry.

8. Ars Quatuor Coronatum is the name under which the transactions of the Lodge Quatuor Coronatum, No. 2076, London, the premier literary Lodge of the world, are published in annual volumes, beginning with 1888.

9. William Shakespeare in one of his historical plays is the author of the quotation from the 3rd Degree lecture, "Thus wastes man...".

10. In Greek and Hebrew alpha and aleph are the first letters in the alphabet.

11. The "Seven Wonders of the Ancient World" are: The Egyptian Pyramids and Sphinx; the Hanging Gardens of Babylon; the Temple of Diana at Ephesus; the Stature of Jupiter Olympus; Mausolus' Tomb; the Pharos at Alexandria, and the Colossus of Rhodes

12. There is a record of the use of the word Free Mason in literature prior to the formation of the Grand Lodge in London in 1717. William Boude, a Bachelor of Divinity, was the author of a book found by W.J. Williams in the British Museum, printed in 1524, entitled "Ars Quatuor Coronatorum" in which the words Apprentices and Free Mason are both used.

13. The trade of architecture was displaced in the fifteenth century as the recorder of history by the invention of printing.

14. Between forty and fifty appendant modern organizations have Masonic Membership as a requisite for admission.

15. The Masonic Calendar is derived from the fact that Masons in America and England date from the creation of the world, calling it "Anno Lucis", which they abbreviate

A.L., signifying, in the year of light . It's as simple as adding 4000 to the year. For example, the year AD 2024 is A.L. 6024.

16. The records of the Masons' Company of London go back as far as AD 1620. The historian Condor gives its establishment as far back as AD 1220 or possibly even earlier.

17. The first native born American to be made a Mason was Jonathan Belcher. He was born in Boston in 1681 and graduated from Harvard in 1699. During a visit to England, he received his Masonic Degrees in 1704. He later became governor of Massachusetts and New Hampshire.

18. The oldest thing in the Western Hemisphere of Masonic interest is a flat slab of rock found on the shore of Goat Island in Annapolis Basin of Nova Scotia. On it is the cut date 1606 with the emblem of the square and compass. Various theories have been advanced as to its origin, but no definite answer has yet to be found.

19. The oldest Masonic document in the Western Hemisphere is the ledger of St. John's Lodge in Philadelphia, Pennsylvania for the year 1731.

20. Masons held meetings in the Colonies prior to receiving dispensations from the Grand Lodge in London. Benjamin Franklin published in his own paper that several Lodges were meeting regularly in Philadelphia in 1730. As there is no record on them upon the roll of the English Grand Lodge, the evidently met by no other authority than that of immemorial right. Franklin was initiated in 1731.

21. American Freemasonry originally came from England. Dispensations and Charters were all granted from England during the early years. Later Irish and Scotch Grand Lodges granted Warrants and many of the military Lodge warrants were issued from the Grand Lodge of Ireland.

22. The "First Lodge in Boston" or "Holy Lodge of St. John" was constituted on August 31st, 1733, by Henry Price, Provincial Grand Master, at a tavern in Boston, called the Bunch of Grapes.

23. The first Lodge meeting held in America with a record better than that of pure tradition was in 1720 in Boston held in King's Chapel.

24. The first regular and duly constituted Lodge in America is First Lodge in Boston, July 30th, 1733

25. The date of the oldest existing Masonic record in America is the First Lodge in Boston, December 27th, 1738.

26. There Lodges were formed in Massachusetts by Grand Lodges of foreign jurisdictions: St. Andrews, chartered in 1756, by the Grand Lodge of Scotland, Ancient York Lodge - No. 169 of Boston, chartered prior to 1722 by the Athol Grand Lodge of England, and the African Lodge of Boston.

27. The Masons played a big part in the Boston Tea Party, those who participated in the raid were Masons and the entire planning was done in a Masonic Lodge room.

28. The record for St. Andrews Lodge on the night of the Boston Tea Party states, "that the Lodge was closed until the next night, on account of the few members in attendance".

29. Well known Mason and patriot General Warren, who

was the Worshipful Master of his Lodge, was killed at the battle of Bunker Hill, he died June 17th, 1775.

30. John Hancock and Paul Revere belonged to the Lodge of St. Andrew, which in 1764 purchased the Green Dragon Tavern or "Freemason's Arms" as a meeting place.

31. The Massachusetts Grand Lodge declared its independence early in 1777 and established itself as a Sovereign Grand Lodge. This was immediately followed by Virginia, and within a few years each state had its own Grand Lodge.

32. The earliest known use of the word "Freemason" in print in America was in the *Boston News Letter* for January 5, 1718.

33. Benjamin Franklin was a Mason. On June 24, 1734, he was elected first Provincial Grand Master of Pennsylvania.

34. During his residence in Paris, Ben Franklin joined the Lodge of Nine Muses. It was in this Lodge that he participated in the initiation of Voltaire.

35. French nobleman Marquis de Lafayette who was an officer in the American army was a Mason. General George Washington made him a Mason in the Army Lodge at Valley Forge.

36. General Lafayette last appeared in America as a Mason at the laying of the cornerstone of the Bunker Hill monument June 17, 1825. At the close of the ceremony, he gave his apron to Brother Francis C. Whiston of Boston, one of the Marshals, who fifty years later, on June 17, 1885, presented it to the Grand Lodge of Massachusetts at its quarterly Communication.

37. Joseph Brant, a Mohawk Indian who was initiated in London in 1776. While in command of some Indian troops in the British service, who were prepared to kill Captain McKinsty, an officer in the colonial army, when he noticed the mystic appeal in the hour of danger, whereupon he interposed and saved his brother from his impending fate. He rescued McKinsty, took him to Quebec, and placed him in the hands of English Masons.

38. Daniel Webster once called the Green Dragon Tavern the "Headquarters of the American Revolution".

39. The first Masonic public procession in America was May 26, 1737, in Charleston, South Carolina.

40. Masonry was practiced among the Continental Army. General George Washington, General Warren, and General Wayne were all Masons, and it was at Valley Forge that General Lafayette received his Degrees from Washington.

41. During the Revolutionary War most of the Colonies the "Ancients" favored the revolutionists, and the "Moderns" were loyal to King George III.

42. The first Masonic Temple in America was erected in 1784 at Lodge Alley, near Second and Chestnut Streets in Philadelphia.

43. There were ten military Lodges in the Colonial Army during the Revolution, the oldest of which was St. John's Regimental Lodge, chartered by the Provincial Grand Lodge of New York, NY on July 24, 1775.

44. The Lodges in Massachusetts do not have numbers like

other states. Since the first chartering of Lodges in Massachusetts, it has been a tradition to use only the name.

45. The public school system of New York had its beginnings in a modest experiment assisted by the Grand Lodge of that state.

46. The Grand Lodge of Pennsylvania maintained an adult Sunday School, in its temple on Chestnut Street.

47. George Washington was made a Mason in the Fredericksburg Lodge, Fredericksburg, Virginia, at the third communication after its organization, which took place September 1, 1752.

48. Washington took his First Degree on November 4, 1752, in the Lodge at Fredericksburg, Virginia and the records of the Lodge, still in existence, show that he paid the fee of 3 Pounds.

49. Washington took his Fellow Craft Degree on March 3, 1753. (2nd Degree)

50. On August 4, 1753, the record shows that he was raised to the sublime degree of Master Mason. (3rd Degree)

51. There were 4 Grand Lodges in England in the eighteenth century.

1) The original Grand Lodge was organized in 1717 at the Apple Tree Tavern on Charles Street, Covent Garden, London.

2) The Grand Lodge of All England at York organized in 1725.

3) The Grand Lodge of England, south of the river Trent, was established in 1779 at York.

4) The only real rival constituted July 17, 1751, at the Turk's Head Tavern, Greek Street, Soho, London, as the Grand Lodge of England according to the Old Constitutions, called "Ancients" and also spoken of as "Athol Masons".

52. Of the four original Lodges of the first Grand Lodge of England, the only one still in existence is the Lodge of Antiquity, No. 2, it is the oldest Lodge in England, it was one of the four which participated in February 1717, in the meeting at the Apple Tree Tavern. At that time this Lodge met at an alehouse, with the sign "Goose and Gridiron" in St. Paul's Church yard.

53. The Lodge which met at the "Goose and Gridiron" alehouse in 1717, when the Grand Lodge was formed it assumed the precedency as No. 1, which it retained until the union of the two Grand Lodges in 1813, when in casting lots, it lost its primitive rank and became No. 2, which number it has ever since retained. In 1770 it adopted the title of the Lodge of Antiquity, which it has continued to use ever since.

54. The first code of laws adopted by the Grand Lodge of England was the Charges of a Free Mason added to the first edition of the book of Constitutions by Dr. Anderson, published in 1723.

55. The events during the latter years of the Middle-Ages that are of specific interest to the student of Masonic history include: the diffusions throughout Europe of the Roman Colleges of Artificers, the establishment of the architectural school at Como, the rise of the gilds, the organizations of the building of corporations of Germany and the company of Freemasons of England.

56. There are records of the arms and insignias of the different craftsmen prior to the formation of the Grand Lodge in 1717, these are presented by Robert Freke Gould,

in the 3rd volume of his "History of Freemasonry" gives us a splendid copy of Stonemasons, Bricklayers and others, arms in colors, from Masons of Cologne in 1396 down to a banner in possession of York Lodge in 1776.

57. The old Operative Lodges disappeared about the year 1723. By that time Speculative Masonry had become the whole element of the fraternity.

58. The period when Operative Masonry changed to Speculative Masonry is known as the period of "Transition".

59. The year 1717 is an important factor in the history of Free Masonry because it is during that year, due to the lack of building operations, changes were made in the rules admitting men of all professions and vocations. This marks the beginning of speculative or philosophic Masonry as we know it today.

60. The Reformation was a contributing factor to the depression in the building industry in the first quarter of the 17th century when Masonic lodges began admitting professional men and men of other non-operative vocations. The building of great cathedrals practically came

to a standstill, throwing many fine artisans out of work.

61. In 1772 the Prestonian systems of lectures was adopted by the Grand Lodge of England. Between the period of the Revival and 1772 there had been at least seven revisions. Dr. Desaguliers and Thomas Dunckerley were both largely instrumental in most of these revisions. Preston's "Illustrations of Masonry", published in 1772, went through twelve editions in forty years.

62. The following societies that preceded the First Grand Lodge of England in 1717 all had considerable influence on the changes and adoption of the new Rituals: The Ancient Mysteries; The Roman Collegia; The Medieval Guilds; The French Companionage; The German Stein-Metzen and the old British Craft Lodges.

63. There were 3 types of Gilds in England in the seventeenth century:

1) The Religious Gilds

2) The Merchant Gilds

3) The Craft Gilds

The first representing the Church, the second the twelve great livery companies in London and the trade unions of today are nothing but Craft Gilds under another name.

64. Prior to the introduction of the speculative element operative Masons were known by various other names, such as: Traveling Masons, in Italy; Mestrice des Macons in Gaul; Steinmetzen in Germany; Guilds in England and Companies in Scotland.

65.The Grand Lodge made good progress after its organization in 1717. In June of 1721, twelve Lodges were represented by their Masters and Wardens, in September of the same year, Anderson reports the presence of representatives of sixteen Lodges, in March of 1722, it had increased to twenty-four and in April of 1723 the number had increased to thirty.

66. The English Lodges have in additional officers to those which we have in America. In the York Rite as practiced in England the additional officers are a Director of Ceremonies, a Chaplain, and an Inner Guard.

67. "Audi, Vide, Tace" means "Hear, see and be silent", a motto frequently found in Masonic Medals. It was adopted as the motto of the Grand Lodge of England in 1813.

68. The York Rite is the oldest of all the rites, and consisted originally of only three degrees:

1) Entered Apprentice

2) Fellow Craft

3) Master Mason

The Rite in its purity does not now exist anywhere. The nearest approach to it is the St. John's Masonry of Scotland.

69. The Operative Mason compensated his apprentice with food, drink and lodging and other necessities, for example, an apron and a new pair of shoes annually.

70. Rev. James Anderson and Rev. John T. Desaguliers are credited with contributing most to the construction of the the 3rd Degree as conferred at the present time. The material for the degree dates to the legendary period.

71. Over three thousand degrees or Rites were fabricated in the first century after the revival in 1717 claiming to be Masonic or analogous thereto.

72. The early records have we of non-Operatives receiving Masonic Degrees include: Elias Ashmole's, the Antiquary, who states in his diary, that he and Col. Mainwaring were initiated in a Lodge at Warrington in 1646, and he records the admission of several other non-operatives in 1682 at a Lodge held in London.

73. Good-fellowship, morality and secrecy were the traits taught to our ancient brethren for becoming "Gentlemen Masons".

74. York, England has been called the Mecca of Masonry. The record of minutes of Lodges in the city of York are the oldest in the country.

75. The period in history that is generally covered in the term, Middle Ages by most historians is the date of the liberation of Rome in AD 493 by Theodoric to the fall of Constantinople in AD 1453, followed by the discovery of America in AD 1492.

76. The English equivalent to our calling from labor to refreshment is "Calling Off".

77. Prince Edwin summoned the Masons to York in AD 926.

78. Queen Elizabeth in England sent soldiers to the York meeting of the Grand Lodge, to prevent their deliberations.

79. The awarding of annuities to old members, or dependents of deceased brethren is one of the customs of the English Lodges of distributing their philanthropies.

80. The alehouse, Goose and Gridiron, where that English Grand Lodge was formed was demolished in 1894.

81. King Edward VII was Grand Master of English Masons for twenty-seven years. When as Prince of Wales, he was Grand Master from 1874 to 1901, at which time he became king upon the death of his mother, Queen Victoria. He was succeeded by his brother the Duke of Connaught.

82. The Athol Masons were the Masons who, in 1752, seceded from the Grand Lodge of England and established themselves under the name of the Ancient Masons, who in 1776 elected the Duke of Athol their Grand Master, an office which he held until 1813, when the union of the two

Grand Lodges took place.

83. The "Modern" Masons were the name the "Ancients" gave to the supporters of the original Grand Lodge of England which was formed in 1717.

84. This influenced Masonry in America because there was a constant lack of harmony between the Lodges which were under warrants from the Grand Lodge of "Ancients" and those which received theirs from the regular or "Moderns".

85. In 1813 reconciliation took place between the two Grand Lodges of England.

86. The same reconciliation was affected in America when the two Grand Lodges of South Carolina were the last to unite in 1817 and the differences between the "Ancients" and "Moderns" were abolished.

87. The dissention between the "Ancients" and "Moderns" in England spread to the Colonies. The "Antient" work as it was spelled was introduced into Pennsylvania in 1757, the first Lodge chartered in 1758. Pennsylvania work is to this

day that of "Antient" Grand Lodge, differing in many details from that of any other American Grand Lodge.

88. The leading spirit in the Athol Grand Lodge was Laurence Dermott, who was its secretary for over thirty years. In 1756 he published their first book of laws, called

Ahiman Rezon or *Help to a Brother.*

89. When the schism between the Ancients and the Moderns occurred in 1751, the Ancients had a large following. The Ancients were fortunate in having Laurence Dermott on their rolls and he was a big factor in the success of their movement. In 1771, when the Duke of Athol became Grand Master, the Ancients had almost two hundred Lodges on their rolls.

90. The Ahiman Rezon is the name of the Book of Constitutions, which was used by the Ancient Division of Freemasons, which separated in 1739 from the Grand Lodge of England. The "true Ahiman Rezon" was compiled in 1772 by Laurence Dermott, Deputy Grand Master of that body.

91. One of the probable reasons for the popularity of the

Athol Lodges following the schism was the adoption of a
4th Degree by the Grand Lodge of Ancients gave that body
a popularity which it probably would not ordinarily have
obtained. This Degree is now known to the fraternity as the
Royal Arch.

92. The Athol Grand Lodge of Grand Lodge of Ancients
granted its first warrant for a Lodge in the Colonies was
1758, in Pennsylvania.

93. The union of the "Ancient" and "Modern" Grand
Lodges was consummated on December 17, 1813, at
Freemason's Hall, London. The articles of union were
signed by the two Grand Masters and six commissioners,
and the seals of both Grand Lodges were affixed. Upon the
nomination of the Duke of Sussex by the Duke of Kent, he
was unanimously elected and placed on the throne.

94. The term "Ancient Free Masons" has been used in
South Carolina since 1817. There had been a reconciliation
effected between the Athol and Modern Lodges in 1808,
but for only a brief period. However, in 1817 a new union
was formed which has been permanent.

95. The reconciliation was affected between the "Ancients"

or "Athol Grand Lodge" and the "Moderns" or "Grand Lodge of England" were inaugurated toward the close of the 18th century, and finally, in 1813, the Athol Grand Lodge was forever dissolved by a fusion of the two contending bodies in England into the now existing body under the title of the "United Grand Lodge of England".

96. The leading figures in the union of the Athol Grand Lodge of "Ancients" and the Grand Lodge of England of "Moderns" were the two sons of King George III, one of who headed the "Moderns" and the other the "Ancients". They arranged articles of Union between the two Grand Lodges, which were ratified in each of those bodies, December 1, 1813, in Freemason's Hall in London.

97. The Lodge of Reconciliation: When the two contending Grand Lodges of England, known as the "Ancients' and the "Moderns" resolved in 1813, to put an end to all differences, it was provided in the fifth article of union for a Lodge of Reconciliation. Its purpose being to visit Lodges in both jurisdictions to instruct the officers, to establish a uniformity of ritual. It was constituted on December 27, 1813, and when its duties had been fulfilled, it ceased to exist by its own limitation in 1816.

98. Definition of a Cowan: This purely Masonic term is

derived from the Greek "kuon" which is a dog. In the early ages of the church, infidels and unbaptized profane were called "dogs". (See the Holy Bible, New Testament Gospel of Matthew, Chapter 12 verse 6, "Give not that which is holy unto the dogs".

99. Definition of an eavesdropper: A listener. A name taken from the punishment, according to Dr. Oliver, to be inflicted on a detected cowan, and which he was "To be placed under the eaves of a house in rainy weather, till the water runs in at his shoulders and out at his heels".

Freemasonry Fun Facts 100-199

100. Definition of a hecatomb: A sacrifice of one hundred oxen.

101. The source of the term "riding the goat" is attributed to Dr. Oliver, he stated that the English commonly thought that Freemasons "raised the devil" in their Lodges, so riding the goat, which is an alleged practice of witchcraft, was transferred to the Masons. The idiom remains up to the present day.

102. The Halliwell Manuscript is the oldest Masonic document extant, known as the Regius poem it is not only Christian but definitely Catholic. It is dated about 1390.

103. The Sloane Manuscript No. 3329 in the British Museum indicates that Freemasonry is the *symbolic expression of a religious idea.*

104. There are now seventy copies (or forms) of the old Manuscript Constitutions that are a matter of record that have not only been traced, but transcribed, but to these must be added nine printed versions (some of which are fragments of unknown originals).

105. A demit is a certificate of withdrawal of membership. It relieves the member from all pecuniary contributions and debars him from pecuniary relief but does not cancel his Masonic obligation.

106. The following is entered in the diary of Elias Ashmole during the period of Operative Masonry: "October 16, 1646, 4:30 P.M.--I was made a Free Mason at Warrington, in Lancashire, with Colonel Henry Mainwaring, of Karingham in Cheshire. The diary also gives "the names of those that were then of the Lodge".

107. There are twenty-five Landmarks. Until the year 1858 no effort had been made to give them a comprehensible form, until Mackey in the year published an article in the

American Quarterly Review of Masonry on "The Foundation of Masonic Laws" which contained a distinct enumeration of the Landmarks, which has since been generally adopted by the fraternity.

108. The "Laws of Masonry" came under three classifications:

1) The Landmarks.

2) General Laws adopted prior to 1721.

3) Local Laws--These are the regulations which since 1721 have been enacted by the Grand Lodge and are in force only in those jurisdictions which have adopted them.

109. The Dodd's Constitutions was a pamphlet of twenty pages in quarto entitled, "The beginning and the first foundation of the Most Worthy Craft of Masonry... By a deceased brother, for the benefit of his widow. Printed in London, 1739 for Mrs. Dodd, at the Peacock without Temple Bar. Price, sixpence".

110. The Landmarks are group into four divisions:

1) Usages that Mark the Masonic from the Outer World.

2) Usages that Mark the Degrees of Masonry.

3) Usages that Mark the Various Ceremonies.

4) Usages that Mark Official Powers and Duties and Private Rights and Duties.

111. There are 15 points for the Craftsman that are accompanying the Masters' articles, and the first one is-- The worthy Craftsman must love well God and the holy church, the Master he is with and his Fellows also.

112. There are 15 articles for the old charge for the Master.

113. The ritual in every country and every state in America is slightly different, but the Landmarks are always the same everywhere.

114. The six titles are the charges compiled by James Anderson as ordered by the Duke of Montagu, the Grand Master at that time. The six titles are:

1) Concerning God and religion.

2) Of civil magistrates, supreme and subordinate.

3) Of Lodges.

4) Of Masters, Wardens, Fellows, and Apprentices.

5) Of management of the Craft in working.

6) Of behavior under different circumstances and in various conditions.

115. The "Harleian Manuscript" dated circa AD 1600 giving the last eleven of the closing words of the obligation to a candidate is as follows: "So help me God, and the holy contents of this book."

116. Mention of Masons in the Holman Christian Standard Bible (HCSB) in the Old Testament: "You also have many workers: stonecutters, masons, carpenters, and people skilled in every kind of work." (1 Chronicles 22:15)

117. Approximately thirty original copies of the old charges prior to 1717 are still in existence. Seven of these are in the British museum. Five in the custody of York Lodge, No. 236. One is in possession of the Grand Lodge of Canada and the remaining manuscripts are distributed throughout the British Isles.

118. The installation ceremony specifically charges "it is not in the power of any man or body of men to make innovations in the body of Masonry".

119. The Harleian Constitution of 1670 stipulates in the twenty-sixth article that "no person shall be accepted a Mason unless he shall have a Lodge of five Freemasons" and the following article provides "no person shall be accepted a Freemason, but such as are of able body, honest parentage", etc. This is the oldest manuscript thought to the earliest in the use of the word accepted.

120. We find the best evidence of teachings of ethics and morality in Masonry in the ancient charges which accompanied by the landmarks are the foundation of Masonry.

121. The Leland Manuscript is an old Masonic document first published in the Gentleman's Magazine for 1753, Page 417, claiming to be a reprint of an earlier publication printed in Frankfort, Germany in 1748. It claims to be a series of questions propounded by Henry VI, and the replies given by Masons.

122. There are twenty-five Landmarks in Masonry. This is according to Dr. A.G. Mackey, who is probably our best Masonic authority. Some other sources give different figures from four to sixty.

123. There are three copies of the Old Constitutions which bear the name Sloane manuscript, but the most interesting and valuable is the Manuscript No. 3329 which is in the British Museum. It differs materially from the others as it is a description of the ritual of the Society of Free Operative Masons at the period it was written.

124. Definition of the "Returns of Lodges": Every Lodge is required to make an annual statement to the Grand Lodge of the names of its members, the number of admissions, demissions, expulsions or rejections that have taken place within the year. A tax is levied for each member based on this statement, which is called a return.

125. The origin of the name of the Masonic Gavel is borrowed from its shape, being that of the gable or gavel end of a house.

126. Many old Masonic diplomas and charters are still in existence, the form that was originally used as a seal on Masonic documents consists of a circular tinbox filled with wax, on which the seal is impressed, the box being attached by a ribbon to the parchment. However, now the seal is generally placed on a piece of circular paper.

127. The three Degrees in the First Section of both the York and the Ancient Accepted Scottish Rite are the Symbolic Degrees of 1st Degree of Entered Apprentice, 2nd Degree of Fellow Craft, 3rd Degree of Master Mason. These are not only the basic, but the oldest Degrees in Masonry.

128. The reason there are three degrees in Masonry: The Latin poet Virgil is quoted as saying "God delights in odd numbers". Everywhere among the ancients, three was deemed the most sacred of numbers. There are in all degrees three principal officers, three supports, three greater and three lesser lights, three movable and three immovable jewels, three principal tenets, three orders in architecture, and everywhere the number three is a prominent symbol.

129. The men engaged in the division of the rituals into three Degrees are Dr. Anderson and Dr. Desaguliers who were the pioneers in the improvement of the lectures that were made by Hutchinson. About the same time Dunckerly made many additions and subtractions. The fourth attempt to improve the lectures was by William Preston, whose work found great favor among the more scholarly members of the Fraternity. Finally, Thomas Smith Webb, made many changes in the work and the lectures, which is

now standard in the United States, except in Pennsylvania.

130. Gould's theory regarding the growth of Masonic bodies several hundred years prior to the revival of 1717 is as follows: "As far as I can gather", the upper ten, "so to speak, among the building trades gathered themselves together in more regular and elaborately constituted bodies about the close of the fourteenth and beginning of the 15th centuries, in both Germany and England, and at the same time began, in the latter country, to be called Freemasons."

131. Gould tells that from 1730 to 1738 the evolution of a single degree developed into the present system of three degrees when candidates were admitted into Masonry according to the old system as well as the new, and that until the publications of the Constitution of 1738, there is not a scrap of evidence from which we may infer that the three degrees of Masonry were practiced with the sanction (or recognition) of the earliest of Grand Lodges, either express or implied.

132. The reason why Lodges all over the world except on special occasions meet at night is because in this selection of the hours of night and darkness for initiation, the usual coincidence will be found in the ceremonies of Freemasonry and those of the Ancient Mysteries. This

practice was almost universal from the Druids of Britain and Gaul to the Mystics of Persia and India.

133. The previous ruling factor concerning the time of opening of the Lodges is that the opening was regulated by the seasons of the moon.

134. This custom originated in order that all Lodges, when feasible should open and work during similar periods to signify the unity and universality of Masonry.

135. The Third Degree is called the Sublime Degree of a Master Mason because of the exalted lessons that it teaches of God and of a future life.

136. The first mention of the Masters' degree is found in the Regulations of 1720.

137. The significance of the designation Apprentice, Fellow Craft, and Master among the Operatives is that the titles were granted not because of any ceremony or degree work, but on account of the length of service and skill manifested in the workmans' handicraft.

138. The Degrees of Fellow Craft and Master Mason were originally conferred only in the Grand Lodge, but this was found too inconvenient, and it was decreed that a Master with his Wardens and a competent number of the Lodge assembled in due form can make Masters and Fellows at discretion.

139. The Fellow Craft and Master Mason's degrees were introduced into the work according to Masonic historians sometime between 1723 and 1730 the second and third degrees were evolved, and in this evolution of degrees, ritualism and symbolism were developed, resulting in the philosophical Freemasonry of our time.

140. The Second Degree was invented in 1719. Its ritual had been completed but the Master of the Lodges had not yet become so well acquainted with its forms and ceremonies as to be capable of conducting an initiation.

141. The second degree of Ancient Craft Masonry is particularly devoted to science. In the degree of Entered Apprentice, every emblematical ceremony is directed to the lustration of the heart; in that of Fellow Craft, to the enlargement of the mind.

142. The Fellow Craft Degree was fabricated in 1719. Brother Lyon, in his *History of the Lodge of Edinburgh* cites the minutes of the Lodge of Dunblane under the date of December 27, 1720, when an "Entered Prentiss" was passed to a "Fellow of Craft".

143. The earliest record we have of the second and third degrees being conferred is where Mackey states that we have authentic documentary evidence of the "General Regulations" published in 1723, that two Degrees had been superimposed on the original one. Later interpretations would indicate the third Degree was fabricated between 1723 and 1738.

144. In Operative Masonry the apprentice had to serve seven years before he could make his "Master's Piece" to submit to his Master and Wardens of his Lodge, when he might become a Fellow and receive "the Mason Word".

145.There is not any difference in the Entered Apprentice, Fellow Craft and Master Mason's degrees in the York and the Scottish Rite. The York Rite has sovereign control everywhere over the three basic degrees.

146. The obligation in the Entered Apprentice Degree stresses largely the necessity for secrecy; while in the Fellow Craft Degree secrecy is enjoined upon the brother, he also assumes duties toward his fellows, and takes upon himself sacred vows not given to an Entered Apprentice.

147. The first degree in Masonry, and though it supplies no historical knowledge, it is replete with information on the internal structure of the order, and remarkable, too, for the beauty of the morality which it inculcates.

148. The degrees of Ancient Craft Masonry at the union of the two Grand Lodges of England stated that "pure Ancient Craft Masonry consisted of three degrees and no more, viz: those of the Entered Apprentice, the Fellow Craft, and the Master Mason, including the Supreme Order of the Holy Royal Arch".

149. Hiramic legend was first part of the work in the third degree in the 1700s as the historian Gould says, "the progress of the degree is to a great extent veiled in obscurity", but the by-laws of the London Lodge of about 1731 and the constitution of a Country Lodge of May 18, 1733, would indicate the conferring of the third degree.

150. The fees for degrees and dues in the years after the revival of 1717 are recorded in 1760 as the fee for initiation and passing was about 1 pound and 1 shilling; raising 5 shillings; quarterage 6 shillings. Customarily those present paid something, usually a shilling; visitors from other Lodges paid 18 pence, unattached brethren paid two shillings.

151. The Operative Masons prior to the formation of the Grand Lodge in 1717 did not have three degrees of ritual and no record that Freemasonry before 1717 consisted of more than one degree.

152. The Degrees of the Webb or American Rite are as follows:

1) Entered Apprentice.

2) Fellow Craft.

3) Master Mason.

4) Mark Master.

5) Past Master.

6) Most Excellent Master.

7) Royal Arch.

8) Royal Master.

9) Select Master.

10) Illustrious Knight of the Red Cross.

11) Knight Templar.

12) Knight of Malta.

153. The work in Pennsylvania differs materially from the American Rite as taught by Webb. The work or ritual differs most radically from that in general use throughout the United States.

154. The Rite of Discalceation is the ceremony of removing shoes, as a token of respect, whenever we are on or about to approach holy ground. It is referred to in Exodus 3:5 when the angel of the Lord said to Moses, "Draw not nigh hither; put off they shows from off thy feet, for the place whereon thou standest in holy ground". It's taken from the Latin *Disculceatus*, unshod or bare foot.

155. The origin of the Rite of Circumambulation is taken from when prehistoric man thought that the sun seemed to move from east to west by way of the south, so early man circled his altars on which burned the fire (which was his god) from east to west, by way of the south.

156. The custom of worshipping God barefooted was a common one in ancient times and in many lands to this day, it is well-nigh universal.

157. The Pestle and Mortar degree is a farcical side degree to which none but physicians were eligible. It had some vogue in the middle of the nineteenth century in the mid-western United States, but it is now obsolete.

158. The Symbolic Degrees in Masonry are the first three degrees, Entered Apprentice, Fellow Craft, and Master Mason.

159. An emblem is an occult representation of something unknown or concealed by a sign that is known in all the ancient mysteries the mode of instruction adopted was by emblems.

160. The origin of the word symbol is from the Greek verb which signifies "to compare on thing with another".

161. The "Symbolism of the Temple" to a Master Mason the Temple of Solomon is a symbol of life; to the Royal Arch Mason the Temple of Zerubbabel is the symbol of

the future life. The former - the search for the truth, and to the latter, the symbol of the discovery of truth.

162. The Vesica Piscis is held in such high esteem as a symbol by the Christians because the fish among primitive Christians was a symbol of Jesus. The Pisces in the Zodiac constellation is represented by a fish.

163. The significance of the fish, as a Masonic Emblem is because the five letters of the Greek word meaning fish are the first five letters of the five words Jesus Christ, God's Son, Savior. Many regret its discontinuance as an ornament.

164. The Square has such a universal significance as a Masonic Symbol because the ninety-degree angle is not only a right angle, but it is *the* right angle--the only angle which is "right" for stones which form a wall, a building, or a cathedral. Any other angle is incorrect, Masonically.

165. The phoenix is an emblem of immortality.

166. The pomegranate is a symbol of plenty, for which it is well adapted by its swelling and seed-abounding fruit.

167. The oldest and certainly the most widely distributed symbol of mankind is the Swastika.

168. The Swastika is an ornament still used as a symbol of good luck, consisting of a Greek Cross with the ends of the arms bent at right angles, all in the same direction.

169. Among the peoples of history we find the symbol Swastika recorded on the bricks of the Chaldeans, among the ruins of Troy, the vases of ancient Cyprus, the panels of Egypt, on the stone tablets of the Hittites, the pottery of the Etruscans, the cave temples of India, the Roman altars, the Runic monuments of Britain, in Tibet, China, Korea, Mexico, Peru, and the pre-historic burial grounds of North American Natives.

170. The Hour Glass is an emblem in the third degree, reminding us, by the quick passage of the sands, of the transitory nature of human life.

171. In the lectures in the early part of the 18th century, the Immovable Jewels of a Lodge are said to be "the Tarsel Board, Rough Ashlar and Broached Thurnel". This last

Jewel was a cubical stone with a pyramidal apex.

172. Masonically, the right hand represents fidelity.

173. Through the symbol of the Bee Hive the virtue of industry was taught to Masons.

174. The most ancient and distinctive badge of a Mason is the Masonic apron.

175. The proper material for Masonic aprons is leather. Usually made of lambskin.

176. The apron in ancient times was universally received as an emblem of truth and purity. The Israelites when preparing for their flight from Egypt were enjoined to eat the Passover with *their loins girded.* Job is commanded to gird up his loins like a man. Samuel when received into the ministry, was girded with a linen ephod. David upon his recovery of the Ark, danced before it, invested with an apron, Elijah the Tishite and John the Baptist, were both girded with aprons of white leather.

177. The lambskin symbolically represents among the ancients a badge of distinction. Dr. Oliver says it "appears in ancient times, to have been an honorary badge of distinction". In the Jewish economy none but the superior orders of the priesthood were permitted to so adorn themselves with it.

178. The source of the use of the symbol of the point within a circle known as a circumspect is from the Egyptian and is a symbolic sign for the sun and the god Osiris.

179. The acacia is a symbol of the immorality of the soul.

180. The acacia is the ancient name of a plant, most of whose species are evergreen, and six of which at least are natives of the East. It is the *mimosa nilotica* of Linnaeus and grew abundantly in the vicinity of Jerusalem.

181. Other plants that were symbolic in other initiations such at the acacia is to Masonry are the ivy in the mysteries of Dionysius, the myrtle in those of Ceres, the erica or heath in the Osirian, the mistletoe in the Celtic and the lotus in those of Egypt and India.

182. Midnight or "Low-twelve" in Masonic symbolism is an unpropitious hour.

183. In the obsolete lectures of the old English system, it was said, "the circle has ever been considered symbolical of the Deity". This is the symbolism represented by the circle in the Masonic Keystone.

184. The Masonic symbolism of the gavel and the setting maul is that the gavel is a symbol of order and decorum; the setting maul of death by violence.

185. A Masonic Lodge represents the Temple of King Solomon.

186.The clasped hands represent fidelity and trust. Horapollo says in Egypt it was the symbol of the builder. The origin of the sign is lost to antiquity.

187. The rough Cube and polished Cube in pure white limestone, the Square cut in syenite, an iron trowel, a lead Plummet, the arc of a Circle, a stone Trestle Board and the Masters' Mark are the emblems of the builders that were found on Cleopatra's needle when it was taken down in

1879 in Egypt and moved to America. It is now located in Central Park in New York City.

188. The true symbolism in Speculative Masonry of the Trestle Board is as the Operative Mason follows the plan laid down on the Trestle Board of the architect in building his edifice, so should the Speculative Mason in obedience to the rules and precepts of the Grand Architect of the Universe erect that spiritual temple, that house not made with hands, eternal in the heavens.

189. The symbolism of the blazing star is the concurrent testimony of ancient religions indication that the star was the symbol of God.

190. The three symbols of Hermetic philosophy are mercury, salt, and sulfur.

191. There are three classifications that Makey, our leading Masonic authority, divides the legends of Masonry:

1) The Mythical Legend.

2) The Philosophical Legend.

3) The Historical Legend.

192. The Masonic elements of consecration are corn, wine, and oil. In processions, the corn alone is carried in a golden pitcher, the wine and oil are placed in silver vessels, and this is to remind us that the first, as a necessity and the "staff of life" is more worthy of honor than the others.

193. Tasting and Smelling are not mentioned in the ritual, except as making up the sacred number five. Preston says, "Smelling and tasting are inseparably connected; and it is by the unnatural kind of life which men commonly lead in society that these senses are rendered less fit to perform their natural duties".

194. The "Perfect Points of Entrance" are the Guttural (refers to the entrance upon the penal responsibilities; the Pectoral to the entrance on the Covenant; and the Pedal, to the entrance on the instructions in the northeast.

195. The rite of circumambulation a ceremonial custom is practiced among other people besides the Hebrews. It was practiced by the Greeks, Romans, Hindus and other societies. Virgil describes Corynoeus as purifying his companions at the obseques of Misenus by passing three times around them while aspersing them with lustral water. The procession was always in such form that the right hand

was nearer the altar.

196. Masonic ceremonials that are usually conducted publicly are as follows: burials of deceased brethren, the laying of cornerstones of public edifices and the dedications of Masonic Halls. The installation of officers is frequently conducted in public in America, with only a slight variation in the ceremonial.

197. The old Hebrew covenants from which we get the "Four Perfect Points of Entrance" comes from Abraham, in obedience to Divine command, when he took a heifer, a she goat and a ram, and "divided them in the midst, and laid each piece one against another". (Genesis 15:10)

198. Baptism is not part of the Masonic ceremonial in the United States of America. Confusion about this is sometimes caused because of a ceremony in the higher degrees, properly called *lustration*.

199. The formal procession of the candidate around the Lodge alludes to the course of the sun, from east to west. The candidate must always have the altar on his right side during the procession.

Freemasonry Fun Facts 200-299

200. By the decree of the Grand Lodge these twelve points of Freemasonry that every candidate must pass are no longer part of the ritual, but Oliver gives these as part of the ceremony prior to 1813. The Twelve Original Points of Freemasonry through which every candidate must pass when taking any degree is as follows:

1) The opening of the Lodge.

2) The preparation of the candidate.

3) The report of the Senior Deacon.

4) The entrance of the candidate.

5) The prayer.

6) The circumambulation.

7) The advancing to the altar.

8) The obligation.

9) The entrusting of the candidate.

10) The investiture of the lambskin.

11) The ceremony of the northeast corner.

12) Closing of the Lodge.

201. The "Due Guard" or "Due Gard" is a mode of recognition which derives its name from its object, which is to duly guard the person using it in reference to his obligation. It is an Americanism of comparatively recent origin, being unknown to the English and continental systems. In some old rituals dated from 1757, however the expression is used, but in reference to what is now called the sign.

202. The Pectoral is from the Latin, *pectus*, "belonging to the breast". The heart has always been considered the seat of courage, hence the symbolic relation to the virtue of fortitude.

203. There are twenty-five Landmarks. But it is uncertain that there are no universal Landmarks. Each Grand Lodge is a law unto itself and determines what its Landmarks are.

204. The story of the "Winding Stairs" in the second degree is purely mythological and has no base other than the allusion from the Bible, 1 Kings, 6:8, and its only value is derived from symbolism taught in its legend.

205. In the ancient legends, the death or disappearance of some heroic god and/or the concealment of this body by the killers was called the Aphanism.

206. The old Masonic tradition of Latres is a legend derived from Josephus. The old *constitutions* said the children of Lamech knew that God would take vengeance for sin, by fire or water, so they wrote of the sciences on pillars of marble that would not burn and *latres* which would float. The word *later* is Latin for brick.

207. The word free happens to become a part of the name of the Masonic Fraternity; that is A.F. & A.M. It arose from the fact that during the period of Operative Masonry that the members were exempted by several papal bulls, from laws which applied to ordinary laborers, as well as burdens imposed upon the working classes in England as well as on the continent.

208. The similar legend have we, among other nations, relating to the expounding of Divine Law, like the account of Moses on Mount Sinai are that of Zoroaster, the Persian; Manu, the Hindu; Minos, the Cretan; Lycugus, the Spartan, and Numa, the Roman.

209. The legend of the San Graal is represented as the emerald dish from which Christ partook of his last supper. It is reputed that Joseph of Arimathea further sanctified it by receiving into it the blood from the five wounds of Jesus on the cross, and afterwards carried it to England, from whence it disappeared, due to sins of the people and was long lost. When Merlin established the Knights of the Round Table, he told them that the San Graal would be discovered by one of them, but that only he could see it, who was without sin. "The quest of the San Graal" became the most celebrated myth of the legends of King Arthur.

210. The Masonic response to prayer or benediction is "So mote it be, Amen", it should always be audibly pronounced by all the Brethren.

211. There are three movable jewels: The Rough Ashlar, The Perfect Ashlar and The Trestle Board.

212. There are three immovable jewels: Plumb, square, and level.

213. There are four cardinal virtues: Temperance, fortitude, prudence, and justice.

214. The seven branches of the Golden Candlestick are part of Jewish symbolism, they are supposed by some to refer to the seven planets, and by others to the seventh day or Sabbath.

215. In the old lectures of the 18th century, the *fixed lights* were the three windows always supposed to be in the East, South, and West. Their uses were, according to the Ritual "to light men to, at and from their work". In the modern lectures they have been omitted and their place supplied by the *lesser lights*.

216. In the Mark Masters' Degree the chisel is a working tool. In the English Ritual it is also a working tool of an Entered Apprentice.

217. The significance of the Cable Tow or what was called "cable rope" in the old rituals or Cable Taw from the

German, "Kabel Tau", is its mother, and the tie by which the initiate is attached to his Mother Lodge.

218. The old writers define the length of a "Cable Tow" to be three miles for an Entered Apprentice. But this expression is symbolic and as it was defined by the Baltimore Convention in 1842, means the scope of a man's reasonable ability.

219. The Freemasons made use of "marks" and they were in use by practically all the building craftsmen.

220. The workman's axe swam. It was caused to swim by Elisha. (See II Kings, 6:6)

221. A plumb-line is a line to which a piece of lead is attached to cause it to hand perpendicularly. A working tool of a Fellow Craft.

222. The indented Tessal or tesselated border is one of the three principal ornaments.

223. The three ornaments of a Lodge are the Mosaic

Pavement, the Indented Tessel and the Blazing Star.

224. The definition of Ashlar is "Free stone as it comes out of the quarry", *Bailey*. In Speculative Masonry, we adopt the Ashlar in two different states: (1) as symbols in the Apprentice Degree. The Rough Ashler, in its rude and unpolished condition, is emblematic of man in his natural state, which is ignorant, uncultivated and vicious, but when education has expanded his intellect, restrained his passions and purifying his life he is represented by (2) the Perfect Ashlar, smoothed and squared and fitted for its place in the building.

225. In the symbolism of Masonry the covering of a Masonic Lodge is said to be "a clouded canopy or starry-decked heaven". We are told in lectures that our ancient brethren met in a high hill or a low valley, hence the covering must have been the overhanging vault of heaven.

226. The Holy Bible, Square, and Compasses with the Charter from the Grand Lodge are the furnishings of a Lodge.

227. The three principal supports of a Lodge are Beauty to adorn it, Strength to support it, and Wisdom to contrive it.

228. Daniel Coxe in 1730 was the "First Deputized Grand Master in the North American Colonies". However, there is no record of his having officiated as such. He was a member of Lodge No. 8 in London, at the Devil Tavern within Temple Bar.

229. The Grand Master is addressed as Most Worshipful when presiding over the Grand Lodge (except in Pennsylvania where the ancient title Right Worshipful is used). All officers under Grand Master are addressed as Right Worshipful.

230. The Grand Lodge founded by Henry Price on July 30, 1733, has maintained a continuous existence

231. The officers of a Grand Lodge are as follows: Grand Master, Deputy Grand Master, Senior Grand Warden, Junior Grand Warden, Grand Treasurer and Grand Secretary. Two each Grand Deacons and Grand Stewards, a Grand Marshal, Grand Pursuivant, Grand Sword-Bearer and Grand Tiler. or Tyler

232. There are 51 Grand Lodges under the American Flag,

one in each state and one in the District of Columbia.

233. In the state of Tennessee the Grand Lodge insists that one entitled to recognition as a Mason, must specifically acknowledge God's "inspired word" or as one authority expresses it "he may believe as he pleases so long as he believes in one true God and accepts the Holy Bible as His divine teachings and His revealed will".

234. The Massachusetts Grand Lodge maintains Lodges in Manchuria, China, and Chile. Grand Lodge of New York has chartered Lodges in Lebanon and Syria.

235. The Grand Honors of Masonry be given by the Craft on only four occasions:

1) When a Masonic Hall is to be consecrated

2) When a new Lodge is to be constituted

3) When a Master-elect is to be installed

4) When a Grand Master or his deputy is to be received on an official visit.

236. When the Grand Master is present at the opening, or the closing of the Grand Lodge and all the ceremony is

performed by the Grand Master it is said to be done "in ample form".

237. The property of the Lodge upon its dissolution: As the Lodge owes it existence and all its rights and prerogatives to the Grand Lodge from whom it received its Charter or Warrant, it is a principle of Masonic Law that when such a Lodge ceases to exists, wither by withdrawal or surrender of its charter, all its property revers to the Grand Lodge. Should the Lodge be restored, by a revival of its Charter, its property should be returned, because the Grand Lodge held it only as a trustee.

238. The city in which the Grand Lodge or other governing Masonic Body is situated constitutes the Grand East. A document issued from the Grand Lodge of Massachusetts, would be dated from the "Grand East" or Boston. It is in constant use in America and continental Europe, but only rarely in the British Isles.

239. There were no divisions in the Grand Lodges of the United States during the Civil war between the states.

240. If we have different Grand Lodges, the work in each Grand Jurisdiction differs slightly in the wording. Efforts

have been made numerous times, beginning during the war of the Revolution in 1779 to a meeting in 1855 to form one national Grand Lodge, these were without success, therefore a variation in the work is inevitable.

241. The Baltimore Convention was a Masonic Congress which met in the city of Baltimore, May 8, 1843. It consisted of delegates from thirteen states and the District of Columbia, for the purpose of establishing uniformity in the work. It continued in session for nine days to perfect the ritual and form a national Grand Lodge to meet every three years. Too much bitterness entered the controversy however, and it is doubtful that a national Grand Lodge will ever be established.

242. The were five Conventions or Congresses of Masons held in the United States:

1) Washington D.C., in 1822.

2) Baltimore, Maryland in 1843.

3) Baltimore, Maryland in 1847.

4) Lexington, Kentucky in 1853.

5) Chicago, Illinois in 1859, it was held by a volunteer assemblage.

243. The rights of a Grand Master: The Grand Master is the presiding officer of the Symbolic Degrees in his jurisdiction. He of course presides over the Grand Lodge. He can visit Lodges, examine their records as often as he chooses. He grants dispensations for the creation of new Lodges. He can make Masons at Sight.

244. Only Grand Masters may make Masons at Sight. The prerogative of the Grand Master to make Masons at Sight, is described as the eighth landmark of the Order. It is but right say that this doctrine is not universally received as established law by the Craft.

245. The mode of exercising the prerogative of making a Mason at Sight is as follows: The Grand Master summons to his assistance not less than six other Masons, convenes a Lodge, and without any previous probation, but "on sight" of the candidate, confers the degrees upon him, after which he dissolves the Lodge and dismisses the brethren.

246. Four Americans were made Mason at Sight:

1) John Wanamaker, at Philadelphia, Pennsylvania.

2) Charles W. Fairbanks, at Indianapolis, Indiana.

3) Rear-Admiral Winfield Scott Schley, at Washington,

D.C.

4) William Howard Taft, as President-elect, at Cincinnati, Ohio, February 18, 1909, by the Grand Master of Ohio.

247. The Grand Master that had the longest tenure of office was the Duke of Sussex, who at his death in 1843, had been Grand Master for over thirty years.

248. In Masonic processions the oldest Master Mason present is generally selected to be the Bible-Bearer to carry the open Bible, Square and Compasses on a cushion before the Chaplain. The "Grand Bible-Bearer" is an officer of the Grand Lodge of Scotland.

249. The origin of the wearing of collars by the Lodge officers as an official decoration, is of a very old date. The custom is derived from the practices of heraldry. It was an article of investiture of city and state officers as well as knights.

251. The office of Deacon was instituted circa AD 1800. The were to relieve the Wardens of a portion of the duties previously performed by them. The Athol Lodges began having deacons in the line of officers upon the adoption of

the Constitution of 1751, complied by Pratt.

252. The badge of office for the Deacons are as follows: The Senior Deacon carries a rod and wears as a jewel, of a square and compass with the sun in the center; the Junior Deacon also has a rod and has a somewhat similar jewel excepting that the square and compass has a moon in the center.

253. The badge of office for the Stewards are as follows: They carry a rod, and the jewel of their office is the cornucopia, which is the symbol of plenty.

254. The Tiler (or Tyler) is the Eighth Officer of the Lodge.

255. The origin of the title of Tiler (or Tyler) is that he was called Tiler or Tyler because the man who put the roof or tiles (tiler) completed the building secure from intrusion, so the officer who guarded the door, by analogy, was thus named Tiler.

256. The reason it is called the "Tiler's Oath" is because it was usually given in the Tiler's room and previously

administered by him.

257. One of the duties of the Tiler in colonial times was to visit every member of the Lodge and personally summon him to attend each meeting.

258. United States presidents that have been Grand Master of their state are Andrew Jackson, who was the Grand Master of Tennessee and Harry S Truman who was Grand Master of Missouri.

259. "Jug Lodges" is a contemptuous title, given during the anti-Masonic excitement following the Morgan episode, given to certain groups of swindlers who professed to confer Masonic degrees on men gullible enough to be victims. They derived their instructions from the so-called expositions of Morgan. The customary fee was a jug of whiskey.

260. The definition of Freemasonry is that "Freemasonry is a system of morality, veiled in allegory, and illustrated by symbols."

261. A fine modern expression of Masonry is that

Freemasonry is not a Lodge, it is not a Ritual, but a plan for the living of life and a belief in the fatherhood of God and the brotherhood of man.

262. Freemasonry is not literally a secret society, but an association of men with secrets. The society, its membership and insignia are well known. Music is a secret from the mute, Mathematics is a secret from the ignorant, Philosophy is a secret from the unscholarly mind. So it is that Freemasonry is a secret from the uninitiated.

263. Early Masonic leader Reverend George Oliver, D.D. was responsible for making the Masonic system essentially Biblical. He was born November 5, 1782, and died March 3, 1867. He was the most prolific Masonic scholar of his time.

264. The definition of Masonry given in the German *Handbuch* published in 1900 is as follows: "Masonry is he activity of closely united men who, employing symbolical forms borrowed principally from the Mason's trade and from architecture, work for the welfare of mankind, striving morally to ennoble themselves and others, and thereby to bring about a universal league of mankind, which they aspire to exhibit even now on a small scale."

265. A sectarian explanation of the three Masonic degrees is hardly feasible. While it teaches the principles of Christianity, is legends and historical drama are all taken from the pre-Christian era. Many of the higher degrees are based on incidents of the Christian era, but the three symbolic degrees refer in no way to New Testament history.

266. We indicate Masonically the hour of mid-day or noon as High Twelve.

267. The initials A.O. mean the Year of the Order. The date used in documents connected with Masonic Templarism. It refers to the establishment of the Order of Knights Templar in AD 1118.

268. The term "Domatic Mason" is from a time in Scotland when Operative Masons were called "Domatic," while the Speculative Masons were known as "Geomatic." The reason of the two terms is unknown.

269. Blue is considered the color of Masonry. To the Mason it is a symbol of universal friendship and benevolence, because, as it is the color of the vault of heaven, which embraces the earth, we are thus reminded

that in the breast of every brother, these virtues should be equally extensive. It is therefore the only color, except white, which should be used in a Master's Lodge.

270. The first recorded use of the word Free-mason is in the Statute 25 Edward I (1350) entitled *"Le Statuts d'Artificers et servants"* which fixes the rate of wages viz: "Item, Carpenters, Masons and Tilers and other workmen on houses, shall take no other wages for their work, but as they used to do before year 1346; that is to say, a master carpenter 3 den., and another (namely a joiner) 2 den., a Master Free-Mason 4 den., and other masons 3 den., and their servants 1 den., a Tiler 3 den., and their knaves 1 den." etc.

271. History of the term "Gentlemen Masons" is as follows: In some of the lectures of the 18th century this title is used as equivalent to Speculative Freemason. Thus, they had the following catechism:

272. The Moral Law is that the will of God, relating to human actions, grounded on the moral differences of things; and because discoverable by natural light, obligatory upon all mankind.

273. Masonic dispensation is permission to do that which, without such permission, is forbidden by the constitutions and usages of the order and is granted only by authority of the Grand Master or his deputy.

274. The significance of the use of the words "it rains" among English Masons comes from the middle of the 18th century when it was custom among the members when discussing Masonic subjects, to announce the appearance of a profane, by the warning expression, "it rains."

275. The definition of "battery" in Masonry is a given number of blows by the officers, or by the hands of the Brethren, as a mark of approbation or reverence, and at times accompanied by the acclamation. A practice of the higher degrees of Masonry.

276. A good definition for the term initiation is: "Initiation is an analogy of man's advent from prenatal darkness into the light of human fellowship, moral truth, and spiritual faith." From the Latin *initium*; a beginning, a birth, a coming into being.

277. The difference between Free or Freestone Masons and Rough Masons is that the Freestone Masons knew how to

draw plans and lay out work and the Rough Masons were setters and layers. The quotation is given form Wyclifs' Bible of 1382, "Many crafts men, Masouns and leyers." (I Chronicle 22:15).

278. The history of the term Journeymen in Operative Masonry is as follows: A mason, who having served his apprenticeship, began to work for himself, was then called a journeyman, but he was required in a reasonable period (in Scotland it was two years) to join a Lodge when he was said to have passed a Fellow Craft. Thus, in the minutes of St. Mary's Chapel Lodge of Edinburgh, on the 27th of December 1689, it was declared that "No Master shall employ a person who has not been passed a Fellow Craft in two years after the expiring of his apprenticeship"; and the names of several journeymen are given who had not complied with the law.

279. The difference between "Letter Masons" and "Salute Masons" was a distinctive difference in the Stone-Masons in Germany in the Middle Ages. The Salute Masons had signs, words, and other methods of recognition, while the Letter Masons were identified only by documentary evidence.

280. Modern Freemasonry called "Speculative" to denote

the differences between the Speculative and the original Operative art.

281. An Encyclical is a circular, sent to many places or persons. They are sometimes issued by Grand Lodges or Grand Masters to members in the jurisdiction. The word is not in common use.

282. The term "Parrot Mason" refers to one who commits to memory questions and answers of the cathetical lectures and the formulaes of the ritual only.

283. Solomon occupied building the temple for seven years. The construction of the collateral addition covered thirteen years, the entire task consuming about twenty years.

284. The proper use of the initials of A.F. & A.M. or F. & A.M. is about equally divided in the United States. The practice was inherited from the great schism, the MODERNS using the former and the ANCIENTS the latter.

285. The real foundations of Masonry both material and moral are the deep need and aspiration of man, his creative

impulse, his love of light and his instinctive faith that the mind of man is akin to the Mind that made it.

286. The search for the etymology of the word *Mason* has given rise to numerous theories, many of them absurd. Dr. Murray thought that the word was from the root of Latin "maceria" (a wall), but we prefer the root of Medieval Latin *Maconner*, to build or *Maconetus* a builder.

287. Dr. Oliver in his "Historical Landmarks of Freemasonry" declares Freemasonry to be "a system of morality, by the practice of which its members may advance their spiritual interests. It is not a religion, but it is a handmaiden to religion."

288. Freemasonry is neither charity nor the cultivation of the social graces, both of which are merely incidental to its organization; but it is the search after truth, and that truth is the unity of God and the immorality of the soul.

289. The term "suspension" is a Masonic punishment depriving a member of its privileges. It is of two kinds, definite and indefinite, but the effect of the penalty during the period of its existence is the same.

290. The Mason's creed is as follows: First, a belief in God, secondly, a belief in the eternal life.

291. The real object of Freemasonry, in a philosophical and religious sense, it the search for truth.

292. A profane cannot prefer charges against a Mason, the charges must be made by a member of the Lodge, but the information can be given to a Master Mason and he in turn can file the charges against the accused through the Junior Warden.

293. Two symbolic themes predominate in the first three Degrees of Masonry are the search for light and the other is the labor of building.

294. It is proper to refer to a Master Mason's Lodge as a Blue Lodge because it is a Symbolic Lodge, in which the first three degrees of Masonry are conferred, and it is so called from the color of its decorations.

295. The principal religious qualification a Mason must

have is required of every candidate for initiation is that he believe in God as a supreme power, and in a future life.

296. Western Star Lodge No. 107, at Kaskaskia, on the Mississippi in what is now the state of Illinois is the Lodge in the days of Western pioneering that was known as the "Mother of Lodges". It was chartered by the Grand Lodge of Pennsylvania in 1805. Due to conditions of travel in those days the dispensation did not reach Kaskaskia until December 1806.

297. The root of the word Lodge comes from Sanskrit *loga*, which in the sacred language of the Ganges, signifies a world, of which every Lodge is a representation. To what we call Lodge the Persians gave the name of *Jehan*, whence by corruption, comes our expression, *a Lodge of St. John.*

298. The ritual has never been uniform all over the fifty United States. The adoption of a uniform ritual through all the fifty states will in all probability never occur.

299. Ever since the formation of the original thirteen colonies, efforts have been made in the United States to form a national General Grand Lodge without success, but it is doubtful that we will ever have a supreme Grand

Lodge in the United States.

Freemasonry Fun Facts 300-399

300. The Lodge in Fairbanks, Alaska is the northernmost Masonic Lodge in the United States.

301. There are several buildings for the exclusive use of Masonic gatherings, but probably the most unusual one is in the little village of Woodbury, Connecticut, built on top of a cliff, fifty feet in height. It is patterned architecturally from the Parthenon at Athens. It was constructed for and has been owned and occupied by King Solomon's Lodge since 1839. The Temple of Tuscan Lodge, St. Louis, Missouri, is probably the most sumptuous Lodge Room of any single Lodge in the United States, if not in the world.

302. The floor of the Lodge is an oblong square; it is half as wide as it is long. It is patterned after the Ark of the Covenant; Moses had made for the children of Israel on

their journey to the promise land.

303. Lawful authority is the principal link binding all Masonic Lodges everywhere. No Lodge can be formed and work without this essential element.

304. The abnet is a band or apron made of fine linen and worn by the Jewish priesthood. It was borrowed from the Egyptians. This probably was the apron which some regarded as a Masonic insignia on some of the mummies of the Pharos.

305. According to Masonic law, women cannot become Masons. However, in France and many Latin American countries women have been made Masons. The Honorable Mrs. Aldworth was initiated in Doneraile, Ireland in 1734. Another authenticated case is that of Mrs. Beanton, who died in Norwich, England, in 1802 at the age of 85. Both women had acquired Masonic secrets surreptitiously and were compelled to submit to initiations.

306. The decision for a Master Mason to make his choice between the York or Scottish Rite degrees is a matter of purely individual taste, they are both beautiful and instructive.

307. The Scotch word for Masonic initiation is "brithering".

308. The secret portion of Masonry which is known only to the initiates is esoteric as distinguished from exoteric or monitorial. The words are from the Greek and were first used by Pythagoras who divided his classes according to the degree of Knowledge they had attained.

309. A Jesse is a large candlestick of metal, with many sconces, hanging from the ceiling, and symbolically referring to the Branch of Jesse.

310. The definition of the name Tubal Cain is as follows: The English Masons and through them the French have derived Tubal Cain from the Hebrew, *tebel* or earth and *kanah* or to acquire possessions. This interpretation has not been introduced in the United States.

311. The son of a Mason, in England, was called a Lewis. Only a Lewis was admitted under the age of twenty-one but he was eligible for membership at eighteen. Term is obsolete in the United States, though some authorities think that may account for the admission of George

Washington when he was only twenty years old.

312. A magic square is a series of numbers arranged in an equal number of cells constituting a square figure, the enumeration of all these columns, vertically, horizontally, and diagonally, will give the same sum.

313. The Ground Floor of the Lodge represents Mount Moriah, on which the Temple of Solomon was built. It was remarkable for three events recorded in Scripture. It was here that Abraham prepared to offer up his beloved son Isaac; it was here that David, when his people were afflicted with a pestilence made peace-offerings and burnt offerings to appease the wrath of God; it was here that Solomon, upon completion of the Temple, dedicated that magnificent edifice to the service of Jehovah. The Kabalists delight in investing it with still more solemn associations, and declare it was the spot where Adam was born, and Abel slain.

314. The definition of an inchoate Lodge is as follows: From the Latin *inchoatus* meaning unfinished or incomplete. Lodges working under the dispensation of the Grand Lodge because they do not possess all the prerogatives of a Lodge working under a warrant of constitution from a Grand Lodge.

315. The definition of a Clandestine Lodge is as follows: A body of Masons uniting in a Lodge without the consent of the Grand Lodge; or even if legally constituted to continue to work after its charter has been revoked.

316. The term "Clandestine" was first used in a note by Noorthouck on page 239 in his edition of the *Book of Constitutions* published in 1794.

317. The Masonic law in relation to "Clandestinism" for Regular Masons is that they are forbidden to converse with clandestine Masons on Masonic matters.

318. A Lodge is said to be properly tiled when the necessary precautions have been taken to prevent the approach of unauthorized persons.

319. Before 1717, all business of the Lodge was transacted in the first or Entered Apprentice degree.

320. There are twelve Lodges in the Pennsylvania Jurisdiction that have no names just numbers only.

321. Seven is the number that constitutes a quorum in a Masonic Lodge, for the transaction of business. The Old Constitutions and Regulations are silent on the subject, and authorities consequently differ. However, it is generally accepted that as seven Masons are sufficient to open a Lodge and carry on business, other than initiation, that number would constitute a quorum.

322. The custom of the Master of a Lodge wearing a hat is to keep the head covered while all around are uncovered, is a mark of superiority of rank or station.

323. The Junior Warden presides over the Lodge when called from labor to refreshment.

324. With regards to the Lodge of St. John the Masonic tradition is that the primitive or mother Lodge was held at Jerusalem and dedicated to St. John, first the Baptist, the Evangelist, and finally to both.

325. All extraneous ornaments, devices and decorations on a Masonic apron are in poor taste and detract from the symbolic character of the investiture.

326. The "Substitute Word" is a symbol of the unsuccessful search after Divine Truth and the attainment in the life, of which the first Temple is a type.

327. The two Lodges with the largest membership in the United States are the Albert Pike Lodge No. 303 in Wichita, Kansas and Ivanhoe Lodge No. 446 Kansas City, Missouri.

328. The state of New York has the largest membership.

329. The state of Montana has the smallest membership.

330. As early as AD 1600 there are records of admission of non-professionals known as non-Operative Masons into the Lodge of Edinburgh, Scotland. Before 1650, noblemen, baronets, physicians, and advocates are recorded in the minutes as receiving Degrees

331. When Freemason and great sculptor Gutzon Borglum was asked how he carved stone into such beautiful statues he replied, "It is very simple. I merely knock away with a

hammer and chisel the stone I do not need and the statue is there--it was there all the time".

332. The difference between a cowan and an eavesdropper is as follows: Cowan is a purely Masonic term technically means an intruder and Eavesdropper signifies an unauthorized listener. The word came to England from the Scotch Operatives as a term of contempt.

333. The Capitular Degrees are the Degrees conferred under the charter of an American Royal Arch Chapter, which are Mark Master, Past Master, Most Excellent Master, and Royal Arch Mason.

334. The Royal Arch, or more properly called the Holy Royal Arch, is the seventh degree in the York Rite. The ritual relates largely to the Biblical story following King Solomon about seventy years.

335. The title Lodge replaced by the title Chapter April 29, 1768, in England.

336. The word Companion took the place of the word brother in England circa 1779.

337. Joshua is the High Priest of the Jews when they returned from the Babylonian exile, is the character the High Priest in the Chapter is supposed to impersonate.

338. 80,000 is the number of Mark Masters that tradition tells us were employed in the quarries of Zeredatha, in hewing, squaring, marking, and numbering stones for the Temple.

339. The requirements for the initiation in the Mark Degree state that it could only be conferred on one having previously received the degree of Fellow Craft and Master.

340. The earliest record of the Mark Degree being conferred bears the date of January 7, 1778.

341. The origin of the name Mark Master is veiled in obscurity, but it sprang into existence in the earlier period of Speculative Masonry. It was customary for the operative to select a Mark, to be placed on every piece of work wrought by them, in order that a check could be made by the Overseer, and to facilitate the payment of wages.

342. In the Chapter Degree of Mark Master the chisel as a working tool symbolizes the effect of education on the human mind.

343. Mark Masons were used in the construction of all the ancient buildings to indicate which artisan had done the work.

344. The Chapter Degrees of "Mark" and "Most Excellent" are not shown in the early records for any recognition as preparatory Degrees. The "Most Excellent" was first conferred on April 17, 1807, and the "Mark" on July 20, 1818. They were not even obligatory then, but appear to have been taken or not, at the choice of the candidate.

345. The Past Master's degree is the second in the series of the Chapter, hence arose the terms, Actual Past Master and Virtual Past Master, the latter meaning on who had received the degree in the Chapter but had not been elected or served as Master of a Lodge. A Virtual Past Master is not recognized in the Grand Lodge as a Past Master.

346. The Most Excellent Master's Degree was conferred by St. Andrew's Chapter, Boston, Massachusetts from 1769 to 1797.

347. The Chapter Degrees can date their birth from 1723 to 1760.

348. The earliest record of minutes of a Royal Arch meeting are the records of York Chapter, June 12, 1765.

349. The earliest date of the use of the words "Royal Arch Chapter" in St. Andrews Chapter are shown in the Secretary's record of the minutes of the meeting of January 30, 1794.

350. The Royal Arch Chapter did not use the present titles for its line of officers from the beginning. The records of St. Andrew's Chapter in Boston, instituted August 28, 1769, show the three highest officers as Master, Senior Warden, and Junior Warden. The same titles were used in the election on April 17, 1770. Due to the difficulties preceding and during the Revolution, no further election was recorded until October 21, 1790. The earliest record of the titles of High Priest, King and Scribe occur April 1, 1789, in St. Andrew's Chapter.

351. The early history of the Royal Arch Degree is lost in

obscurity, but in the opinion of the late Brother W.J. Hughan its origin may be ascribed to the fourth decade of the eighteenth century. Mention of it occurs in the account of the meeting of a Lodge (No. 21) at Youghal, in Ireland, in 1743, when the members......

352. Originally an indispensable necessary qualification for the attainment of the Royal Arch Degree was that the candidate should be a Past Master. As the restriction to those only who had presided for twelve months over a Symbolic Lodge, circumscribed the candidates within a very narrow limit, the ceremony of passing the chair was invented, by which the candidate became a "Virtual Past Master" in contradistinction to an "Actual Past Master".

353. The four Royal Arch Banners are as follows:

1) An eagle, on a blue banner representing the tribe of Dan.

2) A man, on a purple banner representing the tribe of Reuben.

3) An ox, on a scarlet banner representing the tribe of Ephraim.

4) A lion, on a white banner representing the tribe of Judah.

The last one being borne by the Royal Arch Captain, and

the other three by the Grand Masters of the first, second and third veils.

354. Red, scarlet or crimson is the appropriate color of the Royal Arch Degree, for it is called by each of these names and it is said symbolically to represent the ardor and zeal, which should actuate all who are in possession of that sublime portion of Masonry.

355. The Principal Sojourner is an officer in the Royal Arch Chapter whose duties are like those of a Senior Deacon in a Symbolic Lodge.

356. The Scribe is the third officer in a Royal Arch Chapter and is the representative of Haggai.

357. Haggai, who in the American Rite of the Royal Arch is called the Scribe, in the English system receives the title of *Prophet* in the ritual of the Royal Arch Degree and hence in the order of precedence, he is placed above the High Priest.

358. The crow is an iron bar used to raise heavy items. It is a working tool of a Royal Arch Mason, and symbolically teaches him to raise his thoughts above the corrupting

influence of worldly mindedness.

359. Two of the twelve tribes of Israel, Judah, and Benjamin, returned to Jerusalem with Zerubbabel for the rebuilding of the Temple.

360. An assemblage of Royal Arch Masons is known as a convocation.

361. Thomas Smith Webb is the founder of the General Grand Chapter in the United States. He was the son of English parents who had come to America several years prior to his birth, which was October 13, 1771. He received the primary Degrees in Keene, New Hampshire in 1792. After moving to Albany, New York, he became active in the Chapter of Royal Arch and Commandery of the Temple. In 1797 he published his first Freemason's Monitor. While using Preston's work as a model, he changed the arrangements of the lectures to make them more "agreeable to the present mode of working'. His influence over Masonry is to be ascribed almost wholly to his personal contact with them and his oral teachings. He seems though to be the author of a Masonic system now universally practiced in the United States. He died in Cleveland, Ohio, July 6, 1819.

362. The first Grand Chapter organized in the United States was in Hartford, Connecticut in 1798. There was also one formed in Pennsylvania in 1795 that was merely an instrument of the Grand Lodge, who alone could sanction the holding of a Chapter.

363. The four states that were represented at the formation of the Grand Chapter at Hartford, Connecticut in 1798 were Massachusetts, Rhode Island, Connecticut, and New York.

364. The Degrees of Royal and Select Master are known as the Cryptic Degrees. Some modern Ritualists have added the Degree of Super-excellent Master, now, often conferred in a Cryptic Council, but its legend has no connection with the crypt or secret vault.

365. Several attempts have been made to have the Degrees of Royal and Select Masters incorporated as preparatory steps in the Capitular system but have failed adoption.

366. Zerubbable was the builder of the Second Temple at Jerusalem. Along with the High Priest Joshua and Haggai the Scribe he led the Jews back to Jerusalem. The Second Temple was completed in 515 BC.

367. The staff of the Prelate is the degree of the Grand
Pontiff.

368. The first printed record of the Degree of Order of
Knight Templar being conferred was at the Lodge, styled
St. Andrews Royal Arch Lodge, held its first recorded
meeting August 28, 1769, in Mason's Hall, Boston, and the
record of that meeting contains the first account of the
conferring of the Order of Knight Templar that has not yet
been discovered in manuscript or print.

369. Three distinct periods of the history of Templary in
America are divided as follows:

1) Between the years 1769-1816 covering the date prior to
the organization of the Grand Encampment.

2) Between the years 1816-1856 the period of General
Grand Encampment.

3) Between 1856 to the Grand Commanderies and since
the adoption of the present constitution.

370. Which is proper: Knights Templar or Knight
Templars? Knights Templar is the form now adopted, from
the authority of the Constitution of the Grand

Commandery of the United States of America.

371. The Recorder is an officer in the Commandery of Knights Templar and a Council of Royal and Select Masters, equivalent to a Secretary in a blue Lodge.

372. There are over 555,000 conferred Knights Templar in the United States.

373. An embrace on the conferring of Knighthood is known as an accolade.

374. Commandery, Grand Commandery, and the Grand Encampment are the meetings of congregations of Knights Templar in the United States. The national meetings held every three years are called Grand Commandery. When three or more Commanderies are instituted in a state, they may unite and form a Grand Commandery.

375. The first Grand Encampment was formed in Massachusetts. The Grand Encampment of Massachusetts and Rhode Island was formed on May 6, 1805. Pennsylvania held her first Grand Encampment on May 12, 1797, composed of delegates from Nos. 1 and 2 of

Philadelphia, No. 3 of Harrisburg, and No. 4 of Carlisle. The claim of Massachusetts is predicated on the fact that Sir Henry Fowle, a member had fabricated the ritual which for years was standard in all the bodies, both Grand and Subordinate, within the United States.

376. The Order of Knights Templars, of the Crusade era was organized in the year AD 1118 by Hugo de Payens, Godfrey de St. Aldemar, and seven other knights whose names have been lost to history. They took the vows of poverty, chastity, and obedience in the presence of the Patriarch of Jerusalem

377. Baphomet is an imaginary idol or symbol, which the Knights Templars were accused of using in their mystic rites.

378. The Chamber of Reflection is the preparation room in which the candidate remains until he is introduced in the degree of Knights Templar.

379. The Order of Knighthood called the Order of the Golden Fleece was established in AD 1429 by the Duke of Burgundy in Flanders and was in high repute as an Order of the Knighthood.

380. The closing battle in the war of the Crusades which led the Christians to evacuate Palestine is known as the fall of Acre and occurred in AD 1292 under the vigorous assault of the Sultan Mansour. The Templars, after a brief stay on the island of Cyprus, retired to their different Preceptories in Europe.

381. The Social Order of Beauceants was made up of the immediate female kin of the Knights Templar.

382. The term "cross-legged Knight" originated from the custom of interring a Knight Templar with one leg crossing over the other. This posture is assumed in an allusion to the position of Jesus while upon the cross.

383. The Order of De Molay is a juvenile Lodge called Chapters to which the sons of Masons between the ages of sixteen and twenty-one are eligible. It was founded in 1919 at Kansas City, by Frank S. Land. It comprises two Degrees and its ritual is based on the martyrdom of Jacques De Molay, March 11, 1313.

384. The oldest authenticated Scottish Rite document in

the Western world is the one relating to the Provincial Grand Lodge in the West Indies, warranted by the Grand Lodge of Pennsylvania in the year 1802. An original Scottish Rite Certificate issued to Ossonde Verriere, a planter in St. Domingo, dated October 26, 1764, signed by no less a dignitary than Stephen Morin, which is without doubt the most ancient authenticated Scottish Rite document known, at least on this side of the Atlantic.

385. Albert Pike and Dr. Mackey credit the establishment of the Bodies of Scottish Rite in America to Stephen Morin. He in turn appointed M.M. Hayes a Deputy Inspector General for North America, who appointed Isaac da Costa a Deputy for South Carolina, and through him the Sublime Degrees were disseminated among the Masons of the United States.

386. The first Supreme Council was organized in Charleston, South Carolina, May 31, 1801, by John Mitchell, Emanuel De La Motte, Abraham Alexander, Major T.B. Bowen, and Israel Delidien. This was a transformation of the form "Rite of Perfection" or Ancient and Accepted Rite. The Grand Council Headquarters were moved to Washington, D.C. in 1870.

387. The Supreme Grand Council for the Northern

Jurisdiction of the United States founded August 5, 1813, by the Most Illustrious Brother Emanuel De La Motte, "Special Deputy Representative" and others from the said Supreme Grand Council at Charleston, South Carolina.

388. The most reasonable account of the first Ancient Accepted Scottish Rite body is that of Chevalier de Bonneville forming a chapter of twenty-five Degrees of the so-called High-Degrees in the College of Jesuits of Clermont, in Paris in 1754. The adherents of the House of Stuart had made the college of Clermont their asylum, they are being mostly Scotchmen. One of these Degrees being the "Scottish Master", the new body organized in Charleston, South Carolina, in 1801, gave the name of Scottish Rite to these Degrees, which name ever since that time has characterized the Rite all over the world. The name previously given to these Degrees was the "Rite of Perfection", or the Ancient and Accepted Rite; while some authorities have a different version, Mackey is usually most reliable.

389. The Consistory is the meetings of members of the Thirty-Second Degree or Sublime Princes of the Royal Secret in the Ancient and Accepted Scottish Rite.

390. The Ineffable Degrees are the eleven degrees

conferred in the Lodge of Perfection, 4th to 14th inclusive. Perfect Master, Intimate Secretary, Provost and Judge, Intendant of the Building, Master Elect of Nine, Master Elect of Fifteen, Sublime Master Elected, Grand Master Architect, Master of the Ninth Arch and Grand Elect Master.

391. The Sublime Masons are the initiates into the Fourteenth Degree of the Ancient Accepted Rite. The form, "Grand, Elect, Perfect, and Sublime Mason" is the term generally employed.

392. The Ancient Historical and Traditional Degrees are the two Degrees conferred in a Council, Princes of Jerusalem 15th and 16th, Knight of the East or Sword and Prince of Jerusalem.

393. The Apocalyptic and Christian Degrees are the two Degrees conferred in a Chapter of Rose Croix de H-R-D-M (Heredom) 17th and 18th, Knight of the East and West and Knight of the Rose Croix de H-R-D-M. They are founded on the revelations of St. John, whose symbol and machinery of the initiation are derived from that work.

394. The Modern Historical, Chivalric and Philosophical

Degrees are as follows:

19th Degree - Grand Pontiff

20th Degree - Master ad Vitam

21st Degree - Patriarch Noachite

22nd Degree - Prince of Libanus

23rd Degree - Chief of the Tabernacle

24th Degree - Prince of the Tabernacle

25th Degree - Knight of the Brazen Serpent

26th Degree - Prince of Mercy

27th Degree - Commander of the Temple

28th Degree - Knight of the Sun

29th Degree - Knight of St. Andrew

30th Degree - Grand Elect Kadosh or Knight of the White and Black Eagle

31st Degree - Grand Inspector Inquisitor Commander

32nd Degree - Sublime Prince of the Royal Secret, this Degree is conferred in a Consistory, Sublime Princes of the Royal Secret, 32nd Degree.

NOTE: OFFICIAL GRADES

33rd Degree - Sovereign Grand Inspector General, conferred only by the SUPREME COUNCIL, 33rd Degree, and upon those who may be elected to receive it by that high body which assembles yearly.

395. "Spes mea in Deo est" is the motto of the Thirty-second Degree of the Ancient and Accepted Scottish Rite, which translated means "My hope is in God".

396. A "chasuble" is the outer dress which is worn by the priest at the altar services and is an imitation of the old Roman toga. It is used in the ceremonial of the Rose Croix Degree.

397. Atossa was the daughter of King Cyrus of Persia and the mother of Xerxes. Referred to in the 16th Degree of the Scottish Rite.

398. The title "Illustrious" is reserved for all those who have taken the Ancient and Accepted Scottish Rite 32nd or 33rd Degrees.

399. The Grand Pontiff is the 19th Degree of the Ancient Scottish Rite and is occupied in an examination of the

Apocalyptic mysteries of the New Jerusalem.

Freemasonry Fun Facts 400-400

400. The wearing of white gloves, symbolized by a ceremony, the doctrine of clean hands as the sign of a pure heart. In the higher degrees this is sometimes called "Masonic Baptism".

401. The 21st Degree of the Ancient and Accepted Scottish Rite, called by its possessors not a degree, but "the very Ancient Order of Noachites".

402. An allocution is an address of the presiding officer of a Supreme Council of Ancient Accepted Scottish Rite. The word's origin is from the Roman practice of generals addressing their troops, called allocutions.

403. The Reformed Rite is a Rite established in 1782 by a convention of Masons under the presidency of the Duke of Brunswick who was elected Grand Master. It spread rapidly through Germany, France, Italy and Switzerland; its supreme body being situated in Zurich. The Rite consisted of five degrees.

404. The Rosaic Rite is a Rite instituted in Germany by M. Rosa, a Lutheran clergyman. It was at first very popular but was superseded by the Strict Observant Rite of Baron Hunde.

405. The Grand Scotch Knight of Saint Andrew is the 29th Degree of the Ancient and Accepted Scottish Rite found on a legend of the Chevalier Ramsey.

406. The probable date of the first official use of the double headed eagle and its meaning was in 1758, when the council of Emperors of the East and West was established in Paris. It referred to the double jurisdiction which this council claimed.

407. The Latin word Illuminati used Masonically signifies *the enlightened*, often applied in Latin diplomas as an appellation of honor in Masonry.

408. Robert Morris introduced the Order of the Eastern Star in 1885.

409. The Eastern Star was taken from France, where it was known as "Adoptive Masonry". In 1744, the Grand Orient of France called it the "Rite of Adoption".

410. French Adoptive Masonry never came to America. Though modifications of the Degree were conferred at the close of the 18th century.

411. Androgynous Masonry are the Five Degrees of the Eastern Star. It is claimed that Josephine, when the wife of Napoleon, as First Consul patronized the "Loges d'Adoption", the original order, from which the Eastern Star originated.

412. The author of the Eastern Star Ritual is Robert Morris, one of the "poet laureates" of Masonry. He had received his Masonic Degrees in Oxford, Mississippi and while sick in 1850, he had done considerable reading of the Holy Scriptures, from which he received his inspiration. He chose five female characters, upon whose virtues he found

to be so interesting and dramatic in manner.

413. The publisher of the *Manual* which gave so great a stimulus to the growth of the Eastern Star is Robert Macoy, of New York. He published it in 1866, the year Morris started off on a trip to the Holy Land.

414. The Eastern Star banned from Pennsylvania by Right Worshipful Grand Master John S. Sell. He issued an edict in 1821 forbidding members of the Masonic Fraternity in Pennsylvania from joining the Eastern Star and compelling those who already were members to resign. The edict has never been revoked.

415. Ruth, Esther, Martha, Electa, and Jephthah's daughter are the titles of the five degrees of the Eastern Star.

416. Until 1921 the Order of Amaranth was an adjunct of the Eastern Star. Like the Eastern Star its membership is limited to Masons and female relatives. The name is taken from a Greek flower, signifying a blossom that never withers, representing immortality.

417. Membership in the Eastern Star forbidden to Masons

in the American state of Pennsylvania and is also banned in England.

418. Job's daughters is a feminine order composed of girls between the ages of thirteen and twenty who are related to Master Masons. It was founded in 1922 by Mrs. Ethel T. Wead Mick of Cleveland, Ohio. The scheme of its ritual has reference to Job 42:15, in the Old Testament.

419. The Order of Rainbow for Girls is a feminine order for girls of Masonic kinship which is international in scope, even as far as Australia. It started in 1921 in McAlester, Oklahoma.

420. The Amaranth is a Royal and Exalted Degree in the Rite of Adoption. It is a female degree, and it is claimed to have been created by Christina, Queen of Sweden, in 1658, to honor an attendant at her court, the beautiful Lady Amaranta. The Eastern Star is the basis of the Degrees.

421. The "Heroines of Jericho" is a Ladies' appendant degree, claimed to be the oldest of all Female Degrees. The Degree is founded on the friendship existing between Ruth and Naomi. They operate in courts with ten officers and confer three Degrees. Not conferred in a Lodge, but

usually at the house of some Royal Arch Mason. It cannot be conferred by any Mason on his own wife.

422. The fraternity known as the Crusaders is a feminine auxiliary of the Knights Templar. Its ceremonial is composed of a narrative of the mother of Constantine the Great and her pilgrimage to the Holy Land.

423. When the White Shrine of Jerusalem was formed it was incorporated in Illinois on June 10, 1895. This is another organization for the "gentler sex". In their ceremonies they call themselves sojourners.

424. The Holy Bible is the most important book a Masonic student can study.

425. The Bible was originally written in the following languages: Hebrew, Chaldean, and Greek. Christ spoke Aramaic, but the New Testament was written in Greek and Abraham originally came from Chaldea.

426. VITRIOL or V.I.T.R.I.O.L. is an acronym written on the rear wall of a "Chamber of Reflection" it stands for Vista Interiora Terrae, Rectificando Invenies Occultum

Lapidem which translate to the following: Visit the interior of the earth, and by rectifying, you will find the hidden stone.

427. In ancient times Egypt was the cradle of all the Pagan mysteries. Egypt was in possession of all the learning and religion that was to be found in the world. It extended to other nations the influence of its sacred rites and esoteric doctrines.

428. Whether Hermes was a man or a myth no one knows for sure, but he was a great figure in the Egyptian Mysteries and was called the Father of Wisdom.

429. In the Egyptian mysteries the Globe represents a symbol of the Supreme Being. Among the early Mexican people, it represented Universal power.

430. Khufu built the Pyramid of Gizeh and for the study of the stars.

431. Amen Ra was the name of the Egyptian sun-God.

432. Most of our Masonic symbols are taken from the Egyptians, who formed the world's oldest civilization.

433. The sibyls were Egyptian priestesses who were supposed to have supernatural knowledge.

434. Naos was the ark of the Egyptian gods. In its proportions unlike the Ark of the Covenant. The Egyptian gods were reputed to be concealed in the interior of the Naos of the sacred barks, behind hermetically closed doors.

435. The clepsydra is a device for measuring time by a graduated flow of water through an aperture in its mechanism, or a water clock.

436. Aldebaran was a star of the first magnitude.

437. The Copts were natives of Egypt. Descendants of Ham, one of Noah's three sons.

438. Denderah is a ruined town of upper Egypt. It is celebrated for its Temple because of its astronomical allusions on the ceiling of the main portico. The temple

dates from the period of Cleopatra.

439. Crux Ansata, meaning the cross with the handle. It was used by the Egyptians and was a symbol of immortality.

440. The foundation of the Egyptian belief is Eternal Life.

441. Pharos is a lighthouse.

442. Cleopatra's needle is a famous obelisk, now in Central Park, New York City. It was a gift to our nation from Ismail, Khedive of Egypt in 1878. Originally it stood near the temple of the Egyptian Sun-God at Heliopolis, dating back to 1500 BC. It was examined by the Grand Lodge of New York and its emblems pronounced to be unmistakably Masonic.

443. The dimensions of the Great Pyramid of Ghiza are at its base 761 feet 8 inches on each side and it is 485 feet in height. It was built of large stones, none less than thirty feet long and five feet square, quarried at a great distance, transported hundreds of miles, crossing the river Nile, and raised to their lofty position in the structure by methods

still unknown to the engineers of today.

444. The Sphinx is a fabulous piece of work, to which the ancients give the face of a woman and the body of a lion. It is found in great abundance on Egyptian monuments. As a symbol of mystery, it has been adopted as a Masonic emblem.

445. The location of the most celebrated Sphinx is near Thebes, in Egypt.

446. The twelve constellations are as follows: Aries, Cancer, Gemini, Capricornus, Aquarius, Leo, Libra, Pisces, Scorpio, Sagittarius, Taurus, and Virgo.

447. The ten plagues of Egypt were as follows:

1) The river turned to blood.

2) Frogs came on land.

3) Dust became lice.

4) Swarms of flies.

5) A fatal infection among the cattle.

6) Boils.

7) Hail.

8) Locusts.

9) Darkness.

10) Death of the first born.

448. The reason the Egyptians used the lion as a figure of the flooding of the Nile is because the seasonal flooding of the Nile occurred when the sun was passing through the constellation of Leo.

449. The architectural custom that is the outgrowth of the flooding of the Nile is the use of a lion's mouth as a waterspout on fountains, reservoirs, cisterns, etc.

450. Alchemy is a so-called division of chemistry, treating of the art of transmutation of base metals into gold.

451. The science of alchemy was also called the Hermetic Philosophy, because it is said to have been first taught by Hermes Trismegitstus in Egypt.

452. The Rosetta Stone is a slab of black basalt, found in

AD 1790 among ruins near the Rosetta mouth of the Nile and is now in the British Museum. The inscription on it is a decree of the Egyptian priests at Memphis, in honor of Ptolemy V, Epiphanes, in recognition of the benefits conferred by him upon his people. The inscription is first in hieroglyphics, or the writing of the priests; the second in demotic, or the writing of the people; and the third in Greek. This stone furnished the first clue to decipherment of the Egyptian hieroglyphics on monuments and was of tremendous value to historical research.

453. Eleazar, the high priest sent the Palestinian Jews to Egypt to assist in the translation of the Septuagint version of the Bible.

454. The Rosetta stone is at the present time in the British Museum.

455. Egyptian ruler Ptolemy II had the Hebrew Scriptures translated in Greek. The Ptolemys were Macedonian Greeks, descended from the rulers of the Alexandrian conquest.

456. Geometry and Astronomy have always held prominence in Masonic work. The study of the latter being

well-nigh impossible without a knowledge of the former.

457. Euclid was a famous geometrician and was born in the year of the world 3680 or circa 300 BC. He was of Macedonian-Greek ancestry and was born in Alexandria, Egypt.

458. Pythagoras was one of the most celebrated of the Greek philosophers. He was born in 586 BC at Samos, and tradition says he died of starvation in 506 BC. He was educated as an athlete, winning a prize in wrestling, which he subsequently abandoned and devoted himself to the study of philosophy. He is regarded as the inventor of the problem known as the 47th problem of Euclid. Students flocked to him from all over Europe, Asia, and Egypt.

459. Because they were so cautious of candidates and especially of foreigners, Pythagoras had to wait for twenty years for initiation into the hidden mysteries of Egypt.

460. The Tryonists were those Pythagoreans who abstained from animal food.

461. The Epicureans were an Athenian school of

philosophers and followers of Epicurus, who were mistakenly accused of self-indulgence to the extreme. The facts are that Epicurus taught their pupils that the best in and of everything in life was for which they should strive.

462. The Stoics were disciples of the Greek philosopher Zeno, who taught that a man should be governed by reason, subdue passion and be indifferent to pleasure or pain.

463. The Magi were the ancient Greek historians so termed the hereditary priests among the Medes and the Persians.

464. The Eranoi were associations among the ancient Greeks whose purpose was to aid and assist the distressed and needy members. It was sustained by voluntary contributions.

465. The forty-seventh problem of Euclid is as follows: "In any right-angled triangle, the square which is described upon the side subtending the right angle, is equal to the squares described upon the sides which contain the right angle". Mackey tells us it is sometimes called the "Carpenters' theorem".

466. "There is no royal road to geometry". This was Euclid's answer to King Ptolemy when he was asked, "Can not the problem be made simpler"?

467. The inscription of Geometry, Plato had placed over the porch of his Academy at Athens is as follows: "Let no one who is ignorant of geometry enter my doors".

468. The Golden Fleece according to Greek mythology was a fleece of gold secreted in a sacred grove, guarded by a dragon. In the Middle Ages it was one of the most important symbols of the Hermetic philosophers.

469. The Doric order is the oldest and most original of the three Grecian orders. The distinguishing characteristic of this order is the want of a base.

470. The three orders in architecture we are indebted to by the Greeks are Doric, Ionic and Corinthian.

471. The Parthenon is the Greek temple, now in ruins, on the Acropolis at Athens, which was built in honor of the

Athens (Minerva). It is the finest example of Greek architecture extant.

472. The Dionysian Architects were a fraternity of builders established in Asia Minor circa 1000 BC by the priests of Bacchus. They are said to have continued their existence during the time of the Crusades, when they passed over to Europe and became merged with the Traveling Freemasons.

473. The Greeks were indebted to the great builders of Egypt for their inspiration in architecture.

474. Callimachus was a noted Greek artist and architect. He is known as the original designer of the Corinthian Column.

475. America's national Capitol building, which houses the congress in Washington D.C., is a very well-known specimen of the Corinthian order of architecture in the United States.

476. The Doric type of column represents the West.

477. The Corinthian type of column represents the South, because it is said to be a pillar of beauty.

478. The Pantheon at Rome is considered the finest building extant, of the ancient type of Corinthian architecture.

479. The Gothic type of architecture was largely used by Freemasons in the Middle Ages and reached its flower in the Renaissance.

480. A pilaster is a square column or pillar inserted partly in a wall.

481. There is only one form of the equilateral triangle.

482. The Triangle is the basic form in geometry from which all other forms are made.

483. Tetractys is a Greek word, literally meaning four. It was composed of ten dots arranged in a triangular form of

four rows.

484. The erection of Westminster Abbey was started in AD 1221, and the building of the London Bridge forty-five years earlier in 1176.

485. Rome was founded in approximately 735 BC.

486. The Catacombs were subterranean sepulchers in Rome, much used in addition to burial places as a refuge for the early Christians to escape persecution.

487. The Roman Eagle was to the Romans the ensign of imperial power.

488. Tubal Cain corresponds to the Roman god Vulcan.

489. The Agenda is a Latin word meaning "things to be done".

490. In the ancient world, in profane history, the most advanced and civilized in the building industry was the

people of Etruria, a region of Italy, between the Arno and the Tiber.

491. The types of architecture the Romans are famous for are the Tuscan and Composite.

492. The knowledge of fine craftsmanship widely distributed through the instrumentality of the Roman Collegia. The historian Marcianus tells us that the Roman Collegia flourished in fifty-nine cities.

493. The Roman commander Titus in AD 70 finally destroyed Jerusalem and burned the Temple, a few days before the Feast of the Passover. He tried to save the edifice, but a Roman soldier had thrown a burning piece of wood into the building and Titus was forced to withdraw from the sanctuary on account of the smoke and flames.

494. The original definition of the word pontiff comes from a corporation of bridge makers and tenders in Rome called *pontifices,* considered a sacred task by the early Romans. Probably from Ponta, Latin for bridge.

495. The Cyclops were a fabled race of giants on the island

of Sicily, having but one eye in the middle of the forehead.

496. The order of craftsmen that Gould, the historian, credits the building of the English Cathedrals, prior to the Reformation to the Roman Collegia.

497. The Sea of Tiberius is the name the Romans gave to the Sea of Galilee. It is seven miles wide and thirteen miles long. It is 682 feet below the level of the Mediterranean Sea. The water is very clear and abounds in many fish. The best-known city of the New Testament era on its shores is Capernaum.

498. The Romans first captured Jerusalem in the year 66 BC under Pompey. He entered the Temple but left the treasures untouched.

499. The Roman Collegia were associations of men engaged in similar pursuits, and prior to the decline of Rome they became so powerful the emperors endeavored to abolish the right of free association. The *"Collegia"* of architects or builders was the last to be broken up when they fled from Rome.

Freemasonry Fun Facts 500-599

500. The Comancine Masters originated when the Roman *Collegia* of architects fled Rome many of them settled on an island called "Isola Comacina" in beautiful Lake Como in northern Italy. What once was only a tradition of the connection between the ancient craftsmen, the *"Collegia"* and the ancient guilds, is now shown by many citations from records to be an established fact.

501. The abacus was beads of balls strung upon rods or wires, used for arithmetical computations.

502. The "arts, parts, and points" of the Mysteries of Masonry are as follows: *arts* mean the knowledge, or things made known; *parts* are the degrees into which Masonry is divided; and *points*, the rules and usages.

503. The Mystical ages in some Masonic rites are three, five and seven years for the Entered Apprentice, Fellowcraft and Master Mason respectively.

504. The definition of Iconology is the science which teaches the doctrine of images and symbolic representations and is somewhat collateral with Masonry.

505. Theosophy is a mystic cult, which seeks a closer union with the Divine, by a higher spiritual development. Annie Besant was its best-known apostle, up to the time of her death.

506. The "Mystic Tie" is that sacred and inviolate band which unites men of the most discordant opinions into one band of brothers, and Freemasons because they alone are under the influence of this tie, or enjoy its benefits, and are called "Brethren of the Mystic Tie".

507. The true meaning of the Lost Word is that the word must be conceived to be the symbol of *Divine Truth*; and all its modifications--the loss, the substitution, and the recovery--are but component parts of the mythical symbol

which represents a search after truth.

508. The Rosicrucians were founded by John Valentin Andrea; he was born in Wurttemberg in 1586 and died in 1654. He was a man of high ideals, untiring, studious and of a philanthropic nature. He wrote a romantic story of a Christian Rosencreutz, whom he said was born in 1378 and died in 1484 at the age of 106. To this man he gave all the attributes of faith, hope, and charity, with a mission in life to raise the moral and spiritual level of mankind to a higher plane. His efforts in his native Germany were less fruitful of results than in England and France, where he found many influential supporters.

509. Robert Wentworth Little in England in the year 1866 has given the *Modern Society* of Rosicrucians its present definite form.

510. The Druids were an order whose rites were practiced in Britain and Gaul, though brought to a higher standard of perfection in the former country, where the isle of Anglesea was considered as their chief seat. According to Caesar, it was unlawful to commit their ceremony to writing, *"Neque fas esse existimant, ea literis mandare"*.

511. The three sacred colors of the Druids are as follows: white, the symbol of light, blue, the symbol of truth and Green the symbol of hope. The aspirant for degrees was dressed in a robe of these colors.

512. Greek authorities suggest that Zoroaster proclaim his philosophy relating to the earth and the stars circa 1800 BC. Aristotle said that it was 6000 years before Plato.

513. The Culdees were the officiating clergy of the Cathedral of St. Peters at York in AD 936, and their prayers were invoked by King Athelstan in that year on behalf of himself and his expedition against the Scotch. According to legend, Athelstan was "the mightiest warrior" who ever sat upon the throne of Saxon England, and "he loved Masons well", but his son Edwin loved them better still, and procured from the king a charter to hold an assembly of Masons at York every year.

514. The Star and Garter was and still is an order that is considered the highest decoration that can be bestowed on a subject by a sovereign of Great Britain.

515. The symbolic interpretation of the phrase from Chapter 12 of Ecclesiastes, "The almond tree shall flourish"

refers to the white flower of that tree and the allegorical significance is to old age, when the hair of head shall become gray.

516. The symbolic interpretation of the phrase "Or ever the Silver Cord be loosed" refers to the beautiful description of the body of man suffering the infirmities of old age we find those words followed by "or the golden bowl be broken". Dr. Clarke's explanation of these metaphors thus, "the silver cord is the spiritual marrow, the golden bowl is the brain'.

517. "The keepers of the house shall tremble" refers to the keepers of the house are the arms, shoulders and hands, the trembling comes with the feebleness of old age.

518. "Those that look out of the windows be darkened" refers to the windows are the eyes. Failing sight is a trait common to old age.

519. "The doors shall be shut in the streets, when the sound of the grinding is low" refers to the doors are lips, the streets are the mouth by which nourishment enters, and the sound of the grinding is the human voice. In old age when the teeth are lost, mumbling is a very common

attribute.

520. "And he shall rise up at the voice of the bird" refers to the bird as the crowing rooster. In old age mankind is more restless in his slumbers, and early rising is a habit with many.

521. "And all the daughters of music shall be brought low" refers to the daughters of music are the ears. The voice loses its strength and hearing becomes less acute in the aged.

522. "They shall be afraid of that which is high" refers to the declining years men fear to scale the heights which in their prime they ascended with ease and alacrity.

523. "And fears shall be in the way" refers to timidity is a common fault of older people. They are filled with apprehension at the first sign of danger.

524. "The grasshopper shall be a burden" refers to the weakness of old age; even the weight of so small a thing as a grasshopper, is a burden.

525. "And desire shall fail" refers to the appetites and desires of youth cease in the declining years.

526. "Man goeth to his long home" refers to literally to his grave. As the poet puts it, "To that undiscovered country from whose bourne no traveler returns".

527. "The mourners go about the streets" refers to the oriental custom of having official mourners, who make public lamentations for the dead. It is even practiced by the orthodox Jews very frequently in the United States.

528. "The golden bowl be broken" refers to the brain is called the golden bowl, from its yellow color. Death prevents its further functioning.

529. "The pitcher be broken at the fountain" refers to the pitcher is the great vein which carries the blood to the ventricle of the heart, here called the fountain.

530. "The wheel broken at the cistern" refers to the wheel representing the aorta or great artery which receives the

blood from the left ventricle of the heart or cistern and distributes it through the body. When this ceases "The dust shall return to the earth as it was, and the spirit shall return unto God who gave it".

531. Theology is the science that treats the existence, nature and attributes of God and man's relations to God.

532. The oldest and most prevalent of all ancient religions was Sun-worship.

533. The name of Sun Worship was called Sabaism.

534. The name of the sacred book of the Hindus is The Vedas.

535. The zenith is the point in the heavens which is vertical to the spectator.

536. The Pitaka is literally, basket. The Bible of Buddhism containing 116 volumes. The canon was fixed about 240 BC and commands a following of more than one-third of the human race.

537. Simorgh was a monstrous griffin, guardian of Persian mysteries.

538. A Yug or Yuga is one of the ages according to Hindu mythology, into which the Hindus divide the duration or existence of the world.

539. The Tiluk was the sacred impress made upon the forehead of the Brahman, like unto the Tau to the Hebrew, or the cross to the Christian.

540. Some of the faculties of the Creator to prehistoric man was Thunder that was his high voice, lightning was His weapon, wind was His breath, and fire was His presence.

541. Abracadabra was formerly worn as an amulet against certain diseases; it was to be written on a piece of parchment in triangular form arranged in eleven lines, the first being Abracadabra and the last letter A or in reverse. Sometimes a form of incantation.

542. The Zend Avesta are the scriptures of the Zoroastrian

religion containing the doctrines of Zoroaster. *Avesta* means the sacred text and *zend* the commentary.

543. The distinguished Mason Albert Pike translated the Zend-Avesta into English.

544. Sir Christopher Wren was the most distinguished member of the craft of his time, he erected St. Paul's Cathedral in London. He was knighted for this splendid achievement.

545. Elmes records that Sir Christopher Wren was a Master of St. Paul's Lodge, which during the building of the Cathedral of St. Paul's, met at the "Goose and Gridiron" in St. Paul's Churchyard, and is now the Lodge of Antiquity.

546. The profane record we have that Sir Christopher Wren, the architect of St. Paul's Cathedral, was a Mason comes from the British Journal of March 9, 1723, it gave the news item that *"the corpse of that worthy Free Mason Sir Christopher Wren, Knight, was interred under the Dome of St. Paul's Cathedral on March 5th."*

547. Delighting in the spirit of worship found in the

groves of the forest was the theory of Sir Christopher Wren, in which man found his inspiration for the erection of columns.

548. The diary of Elias Ashmole is very highly thought of as a Mason record. The other contribution he has made to the literature or history of his period is his "History of the Order of the Garter" which is considered authoritative, and it is regretted that he never was able to undertake the "History of Masonry" which he had contemplated writing.

549. Anthony Sayer, gentleman, was elected the first Grand Master of Speculative Masonry in 1717.

550. English nobleman, Duke of Montagu, upon his election to the office of Grand Master in 1721 gave a great stimulus to the growth of Masonry. 1721 is also the same year that the old Constitution of the Craft was revised. His standing and prestige before the country acted as a magnet to men of broader scholarship and mental attainments.

551. James Anderson, D.D., was the compiler of the Book of Constitutions, he was a native of Scotland, but for many years of his life, a resident of London, and the minister of the Scotch Presbyterian Church in Swallow Street,

Piccadilly, London.

552. The Reverend John Theophilus Desaguliers was called the Father of Modern Speculative Masonry. He was born in Rochelle, France, March 12, 1683, the son of a French Protestant clergyman. The family moved to England as refugees on the revocation of the Edict of Nantes. While he was a clergyman, he was more distinguished in science than in theology, and was an intimate friend of Sir Isaac Newton. He was Grand Master in 1720, and in collaboration with Dr. Anderson he compiled the early form of Masonic lectures, following the organization of the Grand Lodge in 1717.

553. Thomas Dunckerly (born in 1724 in London and died in 1795) constructed a code of lectures, revised the ritual, and gathered all the ancient formulas for the Grand Lodge of England. He reconstructed the Royal Arch of Dermott, and through his influence some of the ritual of the Third Degree was transferred to the Fourth Degree.

554. Inigo Jones of England became general superintendent of royal buildings in 1607 and at the same time was head of the Masonic order in England. It was he who instituted quarterly gatherings instead of the old annual assemblies. This was prior to the introduction of Speculative Masonry.

555. Lawrence Dermott was Grand Secretary of the Ancients following the schism of 1751. He was a man of marked ability and published a book of constitutions which he called "Ahiman Rezon". He also caused the formation of Army Lodges which added great influence on the Ancients. He was Deputy Grand Master in 1739.

556. William Preston was a well-known Masonic author, he was elected to membership and Master of the Lodge of Antiquity, at the same meeting on June 15, 1774. He was a very scholarly man and his work on the lectures was a very valuable contribution in the formation of the Ritual in the 18th century.

557. John Boswell (of Auchinleck) was a Scotch laird of the family of the biographer of Dr. Johnson. His presence in the Lodge of Edinburgh in June 1600, is the earliest authentic instance of a person being a member of the fraternity who was not an architect or a builder by profession.

558. The famous French writer Voltaire was a Mason. He was initiated in the Lodge of the Nine Sisters, in Paris, February 7. 1778, in the presence of Benjamin Franklin and others distinguished in Masonry.

559. Six of the leading Masonic authorities in the earlier years of Speculative Masonry are as follows:

1) Reverend James Anderson, 1680-1739

2) Reverend Dr. John Theophilus Desaguliers, 1683-1744

3) William Hutchinson, 1732-1814

4) William Preston, 1742-1818

5) Reverend George Oliver, 1782-1867

6) Laurence Dermott, 1720-1791

560. John Coustos was a Freemason, born in Switzerland, who emigrated with his father to England in 1716, and became a naturalized subject. In 1743, as a journeyman lapidary, he moved to Lisbon, Portugal, where he bought and sold precious stones. A female servant who knew of Masonic gatherings in the home of Coustus disclosed the facts to her confessor accusing Coustus and brethren of shocking crimes. He was then arrested on false charges and suffered imprisonment and persecution, until released upon demand of the British minister as a subject of the King of England. He was ordered to leave the country which he happily obeyed, and upon his return to London he published a 400-page, octavo volume on his experiences. The book was reprinted in Birmingham in 1790.

531. Two celebrated Poles Thaddeus Kosciusko and Casimir Pulaski of revolutionary fame, who served under Washington were Masons.

532. Ludwig Greinemann was a Dominican monk who while preaching a course of Lenten sermons at Aix-la-Chapelle in 1779, tried to prove that the Jews crucified Christ were Freemasons; that Pilate and Herod were Wardens in a Masonic Lodge, and the Judas Iscariot became a Mason just prior to the betrayal. To subdue the excitement, the authorities ordered him to refrain from stirring up the mob or they would prohibit him from the collection of alms in their territories.

533. The best-known oracle of ancient times was the oracle at Delphi, who neither spoke nor kept silence, but made his revelations by signs.

534. John Paul Jones was a Mason. Born John Paul, son of a Scotch gardener, was born July 6, 1747, in St. Bernard's Lodge No. 122 A.F. & A.M. of Kilwinning. He was a lifelong active Mason, and we have a record of his Masonic activities in the Colonies, England, and France.

535. Cagliostro was the greatest Masonic swindler of all time. The story of his life was published in London in 1787. His real name was Joseph Balsamo, born in 1743 in Palermo. He died in a fit of apoplexy in 1795. He invented what he called "Egyptian Masonry".

536. The names of the "Three Magi" were as follows: Melchior the Hindu with offerings of Gold; Gasper the Greek, who offers frankincense, and Balthazar the Egyptian, with a long spreading beard, who tenders myrrh. The story is graphically told in the book "Ben Hur' by Lew Wallace.

537. "Ernest and Falk" was a series of talks, written by Gottlieb Ephraim Lessing first published in 1778 in German. Findel says, "that it is one of the best things ever written about Masonry".

538. Copernicus was a great Polish astronomer, who asserted that the sun is the center of planetary space, and that the daily rotation of the earth on its axis accounts for the apparent revolution of the stars.

539. Mohammed was a camel driver and eventually became the founder of the Mohammedan religion.

540. The first emperor of the Holy Roman Empire was
Charlemagne, who was crowned emperor in Rome in the
year AD 800 by Pope Leo III.

541. King Tut was a Mason. When Lord Carnarvan's party
opened the sarcophagus of King Tut, January 3, 1924, they
found after the unwrapping of many layers of material,
what has been described as a Masonic apron. Many
authorities agree that Masonry was practiced in Egypt
during the time of the Pharaohs.

542. Raymond Lully was a famous chemist and
philosopher, born about AD 1234. His research resulted in
the improvement in the methods of rectifying spirits and
refining silver. He was an eminent Rosicrucian.

543. The Polychronicon was written by Ranulf Higden, a
monk from Chester, about 1350 he wrote this Latin
Chronicle which was translated into English in 1387 and
published by William Caxton in 1482 under the same name.
Many of the old Masonic legends come to us from this
source.

544. Chevalier Ramsey was a scholarly writer early in the 18th century. It is supposed that he was made a Mason in England in 1730. While visiting the Archbishop of Cambrai he was converted to Catholicism, but later his Masonic writings were publicly burned by the Pope at Rome. His lectures ascribing the origin of Masonry to the Knights of the Crusades, won him considerable standing with the aristocracy, and by many it is thought to have been the inspiration for the fabrication and production of the higher Degrees, notably the Scottish Rite.

545. Frederick the Great of Prussia was made a Mason in Brunswick, August 14, 1738.

546. The three best known poet laureates of Masonry are as follows: Robert Burns of Edinburg, Scotland, Robert Morris of Mississippi, USA and Fay Hempstead of Arkansas, USA.

547. Joseph Smith, founder of the Mormon religion was a Mason. His successor, Brigham Young, had the design of the Mormon Temple in Salt Lake City, Utah patterned after Solomon's Temple.

548. Albert Pike was a Sovereign Grand Commander of the

Southern Supreme Council Ancient & Accepted Scottish Rite, elected in 1859 and an honorary member of almost every Supreme Council in the world. Also considered one of the best authorities in Masonic history and literature. He is usually credited with having composed the ritual of the 33rd Degree.

549. Theodore Roosevelt was a Mason. He was raised April 24. 1901 in Matinecock Lodge No. 806, Oyster Bay, New York. Pentalpha Lodge No. 23, Washington, D.C. made him an honorary member April 4, 1904.

550. Franklin D. Roosevelt was a Mason. He was raised in Holland Lodge No. 8, New York City, November 28, 1911. He took the Scottish Rite Degrees in Albany, New York, February 28, 1929. He attended Architect Lodge No. 519, New York City, February 17, 1933, when he raised his son Elliott to the Sublime Degrees, at which time he made an eloquent speech on Masonic principles and his faith in the Americanism of the fraternity.

551. Mark Twain was a Mason. He was a member of Polar Star Lodge No. 79, in Missouri.

552. Albert Gallatin Mackey was a profound and lucid

historian and writer in all departments of Masonry, unequalled by any man of his period. Born in Charleston, South Carolina, March 12, 1807. He died in Old Point Comfort, Virginia, June 20, 1881. He ranks Gould as one of the best Masonic historians.

553. Thomas Smith Webb's contribution to Masonry was his "Freemasons' Monitor", first published in 1797.

554. Union Officer and Mason, Thomas H. Benton; Grand Master of the Grand Lodge of Iowa, saved the Masonic Library of Albert Pike during the Civil War.

555. The Masonic "Poet Laureate" of the United States was Robert Morris.

556. Dr. Albert G. Mackey is rated the most erudite and scholarly historical writer on Masonic subjects in the United States.

557. Moloch was the fire-God of the ancient Phoenicians and Ammonites, to who human sacrifices were offered.

558. The twelve persons of note in biblical history represented in the Masonic Ritual are as follows: Aaron, Eleazar, Joshua, Jephtha, Moses, Solomon, Adonirum, Hiram, King of Tyre, Hiram Abif, Zerubbabel, Aholiah, and Bezaleel.

559. Jacques De Molay was the famous Grand Master of the Knights Templar at the time of their suppression by Pope Clement V. He was elected Grand Master in AD 1297 and suffered martyrdom on March 18, 1314, with the three principal dignitaries of the order. Fifty-four Knights had suffered the same fate three years previously.

560. "Caledonia, and Caledonians' bard, Brother Burns", this is the toast tendered to Robert Burns the beloved Scotch poet, wherever he visited Masonic Lodges in his later years.

561. Joppa is a town of Palestine about forty miles west of Jerusalem. This was the port to which the King of Tyre sent his ships with materials for King Solomon's Temple.

562. The port of Joppa it is said that the city was founded by Japhet the son of Noah, and from him to have taken the name of Japho afterwards Joppa, and now in modern times

Jaffa.

563. The location of Ethiopia is a tract of country to the south of Egypt and watered by the Upper Nile.

564. Ethiopia is not a good place to hide according to Masonic historians. The selection of Ethiopia as a refuge by the ritualist, seems to be inappropriate, when we consider the character of that country in the age of Solomon.

565. The land of Nod is known as the mysterious land of which Cain journeyed after killing his brother Abel. (See Genesis 4:16)

566. Golgotha is a Hebrew word signifying a "skull". It was the name given by the Jews to Mount Calvary, where Christ was crucified.

567. The Euphrates River is approximately 1700 miles long.

568. Kilwinning is an obscure little village in Scotland which claims to be the birthplace of Scottish Masonry.

569. Succoth is a town of Judea, 34 miles northeast of Jerusalem, near which Hiram Abif cast the sacred vessels of the Temple.

570. The Red Sea is about 1400 miles long and about 150 miles wide.

571. The Vale of Cashmire, in India, had often been called the "terrestrial paradise". The story of this district has been immortalized by Thomas Moore in his poem Lalla Rookh.

572. Lebanon is best known for its cedars, which King Hiram had cut, hewn, and sent to King Solomon to use in the building of the Temple.

573. The river Jordan is about 135 miles long, rising on the southern slope of Mt. Herman about 1700 feet above the sea. It passes through the Sea of Galilee and empties into the Dead Sea 1300 feet below sea level. It has many rapids and falls, the water being sweet and clear. The Hebrews called it Yarden, the descender.

574. The Tigris River is approximately 1150 miles long and flows into the Euphrates River.

575. Fort Hiram was an earthwork erected on October 3, 1814, at Fox Point, Rhode Island, by the Grand Lodge with about two hundred and thirty Masons participating. Thomas Smith Webb, Grand Master, authorized his Deputy, Senior Grand Warden to work on the defenses. It consisted of a breastwork four hundred and thirty feet long, ten feet wide, and five feet high.

576. Shinar is the other name for Babylonia in its fullest extent.

577. Kidron is a brook near the Mount of Olives, meaning turbid water.

578. Como is a city in Lombardy in northern Italy, also a lake of that name. It was the seat of the Comancines or Traveling Freemasons during the Middle Ages.

579. Mount Moriah overlooks Jerusalem. It is almost 15 miles from the river Jordan, 15 miles from the Salt Sea and 41 miles from the Mediterranean Sea.

580. Tyre is a city of Phoenicia, ninety-three miles north of Jerusalem on the east coast of the Mediterranean Sea, and the source of many fine artisans sent by King Hiram to King Solomon.

581. A physician named Brown organized the Roman Eagle Lodge at Edinburgh, the whole work of which was conducted in the Latin language. It was also referred to as the Latin Lodge.

582. The school of Alexandria was a school of philosophy founded by Alexander in Egypt in 333 BC, form which was derived the system of symbols and allegories, which lay at the bottom of Masonic philosophy.

583. According to Preston, Masonry was successfully introduced into Germany in 1733 when a charter was granted by the Grand Lodge of England to eleven German Masons in Hamburg. In 1738 another Lodge was established in Brunswick, under the authority of the Grand Lodge of Scotland.

584. Masonic Lodges in Italy were first organized by Lord

Charles Sackville. Sackville organized one in Florence in 1733, and others were established in Leghorn, Turin, Genoa, and the other principal cities. Due to the enmity of the papacy their meetings are held with great secrecy.

585. Compagnon is a is a French term for Fellow Craft.

586. In 1877, the Grand Orient of France removed the Bible from its altar and erased it from its ritual all reference to Deity. By doing so it was disfellowshipped by almost every Grand Lodge in the world.

587. The French Rite of Masonry was established in AD 1786.

588. The Elu, which may be translated "Elected Mason", is the fourth degree of the French Rite. It is occupied in the details of the detection and punishment of certain traitors, who just before the completion of the Temple were guilty of a heinous crime.

589. The name of the Grand Lodge of Switzerland is Alpina.

590. The Maccabees were a heroic family whose patriotism and valor form bright pictures of Jewish history. The name is derived from the letters. M.C.B.I., which were inscribed upon their banners, being the initials of the Hebrew sentence, "Mi Camocha, Baalim, Jehovah". *Who is like unto Thee among the gods, O Jehovah.*

591. On December 17, 1804, the Grand Lodge of Pennsylvania chartered at Havana, Cuba "Le Temple des Vertus Theologoles, No. 103, Joseph Cerneau being the first Master. Later the Grand Lodge of Louisiana and South Carolina granted warrants.

592. Masonry was established in India in 1765 by an English Lodge at Bencoolen, Sumatra. On Java in 1769 by the Grand Lodge of Holland. And another English Lodge at Elopura in North Borneo in 1885.

593. Masonry in Japan was chartered in 1865 by the Grand Lodge of England on Yokohama and a Masonic Hall was built there in 1869.

594. The Grand Lodge of Mexico was established in 1825.

595. Masonry was established in China with Amity Lodge, No. 407, it was constituted in 1767 under an English warrant and Elizabeth in 1768, both at Canton, under a Swedish dispensation. Both came to an end in 1812, but at the close of the nineteenth century there were thirteen English, one American and four Scotch Lodges in Hong Kong and the Chinese treaty ports.

596. Prior to the acquisition of Cape Colony by Great Britain, two Dutch Lodges had been built at Cape Town, South Africa in 1772 and 1802. Later the Grand Lodge of England as well as the Athol Masons established several Lodges.

597. At one time there were eighty-eight regular Lodges in Australia working under English, Scotch, and Irish jurisdictions. The Lodge of Social and Military Virtues, No. 227, on the roll of the Grand Lodge of Ireland, was organized in 1752 in New South Wales, and after many vicissitudes was at work in the same at Sydney in 1816.

598. The traitors in the third degree are called assassins in Europe. The English and American Masons have adopted the more amenable appellation of ruffians.

599. In India, in modern times, a meeting place for Lodges are called a "Shaitan" Bungalow. The superstition was that the evil spirit was a factor in secret orders.

Freemasonry Fun Facts 600-653

600. The Vedas is the most ancient of the religious writings of the Indian Aryans. It is written in Sanskrit. It is a sacred canon to the Hindus, being to them what the Koran is to the Moslems and the Bible is to the Christians.

601. The cavern of Elephanta in Hindustan is the most ancient temple in the world. It was the principal place for the celebration of the mysteries of India.

602. Belief in God not an essential requirement for membership in Masonry in France and Belgium, but they do not forbid such a faith.

603. The term "riding the goat" is an extremely ancient

superstition. The Greeks and Romans portrayed Pan in horns, hoof, and shaggy hide. The early Christians substituted Satan for Pan and in the Middle Ages the Devil appeared "riding on a goat".

604. The rule regarding rejection of an applicant for membership is as follows: Under the English Constitution three black balls must exclude a candidate; but the by-laws of a Lodge may enact that one or two shall do so. (Rule 190). In America one black ball will reject a candidate, and he can apply in no other Lodge for admission unless the first Lodge to which he has applied waives jurisdiction.

605. During the revival of Masonry in 1718 to secure a membership of good character, the sixth of the General Regulations provided that no man could be admitted without the unanimous consent of all the members present.

606. In the charges compiled by Anderson and Desaguliers and published in 1723, the rule denying membership to women was explicit. This is accented more forcibly by the obligation taken in the final degree.

607. It is possible for a Mason, having been acquitted by the courts of an offense with which he has been charged, to

be tried by his Lodge for the same offense. This well covered in the Proceedings of the Grand Lodge of Texas, Vol. II, Pg. 273 -

"An acquittal by a jury, while it may, and should, have its influence on deciding on the course to be pursued, yet has no binding force in Masonry. We decide our own rules, and our views of the facts".

608. The difference between a Masonic "notice" and a Masonic "summons" is as follows: A notice or notification is just what the name implies and demands neither obedience nor action. A summons, however, is an order and comes under the province of his obligation. To ignore a summons may be cause for reprimand or discipline.

609. "Unworthy Members" are those whose lives and characters reflect no credit on the Institution, whose hearts arc untouched by the influence of brotherly love. They are in the Temple, but not of it. As Dr. Oliver says: "Freemasonry is not answerable for the misdeeds of an individual brother."

610. April 24, 1786, two petitions for applications of degrees were rejected in Domatic Lodge, No. 177, London, because the applicants were not Operative Masons.

611. Amusements that were forbidden to the early Operative Apprentices were card playing, dice games, or other gambling and not to frequent taverns or drinking places.

612. The "Tongue of Good Report" is the equivalent in Masonic technical language to being of good character and having a good reputation. It is required that the candidate for initiation should be one out of who no tongue speaks evil. The phrase is an old one and is found in the earliest rituals.

613. It is said that "A man comes into Masonry of his own free will and accord and goes out in the same manner and is no way obliged to continue his membership for any period of time. Once demitted, suspended, or expelled a man is no longer a Mason.

614. The fifty-second article of the Ordinances of the Fraternity of Stonemasons renewed at the Chief Lodge at Strassburg, on St. Michael's Day, 1563 is as follows: "And in future, in Lodge, no matter for what cause, shall anyone be beaten without the knowledge and consent of the work master. And there shall not be in any employment or elsewhere, anything be judged or heard by either masters or

fellows, without the superior work master's knowledge and consent in the judgment of the penalty".

615. The types of laborers that were not esteemed sufficiently honorable for admission to the stonemasons of Germany are as follows: bath attendants, barbers, gravediggers, trumpeters, herdsmen, watchmen, etc. Article 60 also provided that he must be born in wedlock and his progenitors must be freemen for at least two generations.

616. The law in Masonry regarding appeal is that the Master is supreme in his Lodge, so far as the Lodge is concerned. He is amenable for his conduct in the government of the Lodge, not to its members, but to the Grand Lodge alone. Similar rules are the same in both the Chapter and the Commandery.

617. The provision made in the Grand Lodge of England regarding misconduct is as follows: "If any brother behaves in such a manner as to disturb the harmony of the Lodge, he shall be thrice formally admonished by the Master; and if he persists in his irregular conduct, he shall be punished according to the by-laws of that particular Lodge, or the case may be reported to higher Masonic authority".

618. Four examples of un-Masonic conduct are as follows:

1) Failure to pay Lodge dues.

2) Persuading a man to petition for Masonic degrees.

3) Divulging secrets of Lodge or Rituals to non-members.

4) Criminal Convictions

619. The forms of punishment provided for those guilty of infractions of the Masonic regulations are as follows:

1) Censure

2) Reprimand

3) Exclusion

4) Suspension, definite or indefinite

5) Expulsion

620. The lawful age of a candidate for degrees is not settled by any universal law or landmark. The Ancient Regulations provide that he must be of "mature and discreet age". There is some variation today in different countries. The Grand Lodge of Switzerland fixes the age at twenty-one. Germany at Twenty-five. England, Ireland, Scotland, France, and America at twenty-one.

621. In some states in the United States a man becomes a "life" member when he has been a dues-paying member for 50 years. Some Grand Lodges sell Life Memberships, remitting to the local Lodges the income therefrom.

622. Intolerance is the arch enemy of Freemasonry. Toleration is one of the chief foundation stones of the fraternity, and Universality and Brotherly Love are taught.

623. Persuading a man to join the Masons violates his specific instructions and is considered un-Masonic.

624. These are known as the entertainment or fun orders of Masonry: The Grotto for Master Masons and the Mystic Shrine for Knights Templar and 32nd Degree Masons, and the White Shrine is for the ladies.

625. The Ancient Arabic Order of the Nobles of the Mystic Shrine is the principle Fun Degree affiliated with the Masonic Fraternity. It is non-Masonic in its ritual, but its membership is confined to Knights Templar and 32nd Degree Masons. Its principal benevolence is to hospitals for the care and cure for children of any race of faith.

626. The Mystic Shrine was organized by William J. Florence, the actor, on a tour to the near East in 1870, met the Sultan in Cairo, Egypt. The Sultan, who was the head of a society after which the Shrine was patterned, was intrigued by Florence's wit and charm and had him inducted into the order. Florence upon his return to America had the ritual translated into English, and with Dr. Walter M. Fleming, he became a co-founder of the Mystic Shrine. Membership from its inception was confined to either Knights Templar or Scottish Rite Masons, to insure a "select class of men to compose its membership."

627. The Mystic Shrine began the building of hospitals for children in 1922.

628. The Grotto is an organization like the Shrine, of no connection with Masonry, excepting that qualification for membership. It is the playground of Blue Lodge Masons as membership in the higher Degrees is not a necessary qualification. It is known as the "Mystic Order of Veiled Prophets of the Enchanted Realm." Its main concern is to forget your troubles and have a hilarious time. It started in Hamilton, New York in 1899.

629. The earliest known governmental edict against Masonry was a law passed in England under Henry VI, of

England, forbidding Masons to confederate in chapters and congregations. This law, however, was never enforced.

630. The principal objections that have been urged by the opponents of Freemasonry are enumerated under six headings as follows:

1) Its secrecy.

2) The exclusiveness of its charity.

3) Its admission of unworthy members.

4) Its administration of unlawful oaths.

5) Its claim to be a religion.

6) Its puerility as a system of instruction.

631. The Gormogons in England in 1724 openly antagonized and ridiculed Freemasonry. No Mason could join, until he had first been degraded and then renounced his Masonic affiliation. It was ridiculous in its pretentions and claimed descent from an ancient society in China.

632. In the eighteenth-century Masonic parades were very great occasions. The "Scald Miserables" were a group of enemies and critics that formed a loose organization to satirize these affairs. The first one elicited considerable

laughter, but the more sober minded of the populace frowned on the exhibition and in a few years, they were discontinued.

633. In 1762, Catherine the Great, Empress of Russia issued an edict prohibiting all Mason meetings in her dominions. Later when better sentiment was prevailing, she revoked the order and invited Masons to re-establish their Lodges and constitute new ones. This rule was in effect until her death in 1796, when the persecution of the order was renewed by her successor.

634. William Morgan was born in Virginia in 1776 where he learned the trade of stone mason. His brewery in Canada was destroyed by fire in 1821, when he went to Batavia, New York, where he visited Wells Lodge as a visitor. He was rejected by a new chapter being organized there. With a publisher named Miller he concocted a scheme to divulge Masonic secrets. He disappeared in September 1826, but there has never been any evidence that the Masons had anything to do with his disappearance.

635. Every Mason takes a solemn oath of secrecy, but in none of the Degrees, either of the York or Scottish Rite, does his vow require him to lift the hand of Cain against an erring brother who betrays his trust.

636. Pope Pius IX was reputed to have been a Mason, as was Pope Benedict XIV.

637. When Pope Clement XII issued the papal bull against Masonry many Lodges continued operations secretly and called themselves Xerophagists; those who live without drinking.

638. Pope Benedict XIV issued the second papal bull directed against Masonry confirming that issued in 1738 by Clement XII.

639. Negro Lodges are not recognized as regular Lodges in the United States because they are operating under Grand Lodges which in turn are operating from Lodges whose charters lapsed many years ago.

640. The Masonic authorities and Grand Lodges rate the status of Negro Lodges as illegal Masonically and therefore consider the entire organization clandestine.

641. The Negro Lodges got their work from Mr. Prince

Hall and thirteen other Negroes that were made Masons in a military Lodge in the British Army in Boston, March 6, 1775. They were granted a charter from the Grand Lodge of England on September 20, 1784, though not received until 1887. It bore the name of African Lodge, No. 429, and was situated in Boston, Massachusetts. After the death of Mr. Hall, it became dormant. Later it was revived, but under what process of Masonic law is unknown. On June 18, 1827, they issued a protocol declaring they were free and independent of any Lodge from this day. They assumed the name of "Prince Hall Grand Lodge" and issued charters to subordinate Lodges of Negros in the United States where they are represented in thirty-eight states where they have Grand Lodge organizations as well as in Canada and Liberia.

642. Since the formation of the Prince Hall Lodge in Boston in the 18th century, Colored Masonry has received official recognition only once in the United States by the Grand Lodge of Washington, D.C. in 1898. In a resolution presented at their Grand Lodge meeting of that same year. This action was annulled the following year after protests from all the other Grand Lodges in the country.

643. Friction in the Grand Lodge on the "Negro Question" occurred in 1908 when the Grand Lodge of Mississippi discontinued "Fraternal Correspondence" with the Grand

Lodge of New Jersey and Oklahoma following suit. The Grand Lodge of New Jersey expressed regret and it was generally agreed the Negro Lodge would dissolve due to lack of support.

644. Prince Hall was the son of an English leather merchant, whose wife was a free Negro woman of French descent. He settled in Boston in the middle of the 18th century.

645. Prince Hall was not and never was a slave, his status was that of a "Free" Negro.

646. Prince Hall was enlisted in the Continental Army and served during the Revolutionary War. He served in the company of Captains Benjamin Dillingham and Joshua Welboro, and afterwards in Thacker's Regiment.

647. The date of Hall's induction into Masonry is March 6, 1775.

648. Prince Hall was made a Mason in a Military Lodge working under the Grand Lodge of Ireland. It was attached to one of the regiments in the Continental Army under

General George Gage.

649. After the war, Hall's Military Lodge moved to New York state and is reputed to have taken part in the first Grand Lodge of Masons in that state.

650. Prince Hall and his brethren petitioned for recognition at the Grand Lodge of Massachusetts. They petitioned Provincial Grand Master Joseph Warren for Masonic recognition.

651. The petition for recognition was received favorably by G.M. Warren, however before official action could be taken, Warren was killed at the Battle of Bunker Hill.

652. The claim is made that further petitions were made in 1779 in Massachusetts and in 1868; and that in 1857 Negroes petitioned a Massachusetts Lodge for Degrees, but all were ignored or denied. Later petitions for recognition in New York were also denied because their Lodges were considered clandestine. The Grand Lodge of Washington D.C. took friendly action toward the colored people about 1898, but when such action caused friction in their own ranks and throughout the entire country, their action regarding the colored brethren was rescinded; and at the

present time (1913) there is no fraternal relationship with the Negro Lodges. This although no Masonic writer of standing has seen fit to criticize the Ritual, work or fundamentals of the Negro Lodges and Mackey in history treats of it at length, with no criticism excepting the technical question of its charter.

653. As recently as 1913 American Indians were not eligible for membership in any Masonic Lodges in the United States. However, for many years before this there was a "full blooded Indian" who was a physician by profession, he was very active in the degree work in Chicago and an exceedingly competent worker in the third Degree.

About the Author – Peter Solomon

PETER SOLOMON is a respected authority on the history and traditions of Freemasonry.

He is the former Worshipful Master and Grand Historian of his Lodge and the author of the Abridged Masonic Dictionary and Freemasonry Fun Facts.

Mr. Solomon has appeared on podcasts, radio shows, television, and in major print media.

He lives with his wife Sarah and their dog Pete in Upstate New York.

Other books by Abrandax Publishing / Abrandax Media:

Find out more about Abrandax at:

- twitter.com/AbrandaxMedia
- abrandaxpublishing.substack.com

Abrandax titles –

- All available as eBooks on Kindle
- Most available on paperback
- Many available as Audible audiobooks

10 Easy Ways to Super Charge Your Immune System: Plus 10 Power Secrets to Boost Your Overall Health by Cliff Caswell

20 Amazing Herbs and Their Stories: Fun Facts About Famous Plant Herbs by Cliff Caswell

75 Pounds Down Without Exercise: How I Lost Weight, Kept It Off, and You Can Too by Al Haych

100 Random Factoids: Sitting on the Toilet Series, Volume 1 by Franklin Delphos

112 Random Factoids: Nixon Bowling Series, Volume 2 by Franklin Delphos

332 Random Factoids: Volume 3, Christopher Columbus Did Not Put Pineapple on Pizza by Franklin Delphos

Abridged Masonic Dictionary and Scottish Rite Degrees Explained by Peter Solomon

American Baseball Myth: Abner Doubleday Wasn't The Inventor by Adam Bruce

Aromatherapy in 15 Minutes: The Secrets of an Ancient Way to Care for the Body by Ian Day

Ayurveda Explained Fast: Living To Be 100+ Using 5000 Year Old Secrets of Human Nature and Healthy Living by Ian Day

Before You Sign an Apartment Lease: How Bad Landlords Get Away with Ripping Off Good Tenants - A Guide for Students, Parents, and Friends by C. David Patterson

Beliefs of Reality: Eastern Religions - The Search for Meaning by Thomas Van Lake

Beliefs of Reality: Middle Eastern Religions - The Search for Meaning by Thomas Van Lake

Beliefs of Reality: The Hermetic World - The Search for Meaning by Thomas Van Lake

Books of the Bible: A High Level Overview and Quick Reference Guide by Archer Isaacs

Byzantium AD 330-1453: The Rise and Fall of the Byzantine Empire by Ian Day

Chinese Art of Relaxation: Plus an Introductory Course on Chinese Medicine by Felix Ford

Conscious Contact - Tapping into Your Psychic Powers by Lawernce Paladan

Dry Drunk Syndrome: The Attitudes and Actions That Poison Our Lives by Ed Haych

Dry Drunk Syndrom: Die Einstellungen und Handlungen, die unser Leben vergiften (German translation) by Ed Haych

Fenugreek in 10 Minutes: The Basics About An Amazing Spice by Cliff Caswell

Freemasonry Fun Facts – What A Brother Knows by Peter Solomon.

Fourth Step Inventory: A Guide to Making a Moral Inventory of Ourselves by Ed Haych

Grandma's Secrets: Living to Be 100+ Using Natural and Herbal Solutions by Felix Ford

Healing Power of Black Pepper: The Royal Pedigree of Peppercorns by Cliff Caswell

Hebrew Heraldry - The Royal Jewish Bloodline - A Brief History of the Jews and Jewish Symbols by Ian Day

History of Modern Masonry: A Look at the History of the Masonic Organization by Ian Day

How Christianity Influenced Judaism by Ian Day

How Secret Societies Still Manipulate Us Today: The Real Reasons That Made the Roman Empire Want to Get Rid of Christians - a treatise by Ian Day

How You Can Make Stress Work For You: Stress Management and Stress Avoidance Proven Secret Strategies by Cliff Caswell

The Hoax That is Still Alive: The Protocols of the Elders of Zion by Ian Day

El Engaño Que Aún Vive, Los Protocolos de los Sabios de Sión (Spanish Translation of The Hoax That Is Still Alive) by Ian Day

La Bufala Che Ancora Vive - I Protocolli Dei Savi di Sion (Italian translation of The Hoax That Is Still Alive) by Ian Day

La Tromperie vit Toujours: Les Protocoles des Sages de Sion (French translation of The Hoax That Is Still Alive) by Ian Day

Hydrotherapy Explained in 15 Minutes: Quickly Learn About the Different Hydrotherapy Treatments by Felix Ford

Index of Ancient Texts Relating to the Old Testament: A High Level Overview by Ian Day

The Jewish War – Who Was Josephus Flavius: A Beginner's Guide to Historical Figures and Events by Ian Day

Juicing Explained in 15 Minutes: Plus More Than 20 Healthy Solutions and Treatments Using Juice by Cliff Caswell

Naked Leprechaun: The Power of Imagery - One Image is Worth a Thousand Cures by Felix Ford

No Days Off in Prison: Messages from the Inside by Willie Fastway Wilson and Craig Shier

The Presidents: Revolution by Election - A Quick Overview of US Presidents by William Jonathan Jennings

9 798324 587581